The
FLAVORS
of HOME

The FLAVORS *of* HOME

A Guide to Wild Edible Plants of the San Francisco Bay Area

MARGIT ROOS-COLLINS

ILLUSTRATIONS BY ROSE CRAIG

Preface by Malcolm Margolin

❀

Heyday Books • Berkeley
In Conjunction with Rick Heide

ISBN: 0-930588-46-0

Library of Congress Catalog Card Number: 90-84053

Printed in the United States of America
10 9 8 7 6 5 4 3 2 1

Produced and Coordinated by Bookmakers, Berkeley, CA:
Editorial Services by The Compleat Works
Design by Irene Imfeld Graphic Design
Typography by Archetype 🙰 in ITC Usherwood

Heyday Books
P.O. Box 9145
Berkeley, CA 94709

ACKNOWLEDGMENTS

Nine years after I began writing these pages, this book is finally in your hands, launched into the world. First, thanks to the friends who had the guts to keep asking how the book was coming along. Your enthusiasm and confidence were a tonic. Richard, my mother, and Tom Huntington deserve special mention: they each talked about the book in a way that was uniquely heartening. Martha Casselman was the first professional to like my writing, and her efforts on behalf of my first manuscript helped me take the whole business seriously enough to keep going. Ruth Stevenson gave me energetic and delightful companionship on many of my field trips.

When the book was only an idea and I was unsure of whether to pursue it, my sister Alice told me that one way to evaluate a dream is to decide what the worst possible outcome could be and whether you could stand it. Then, if you pursue the dream, you have the strength that comes from knowing that failure won't be the end of the world. It turned out to be unusually helpful advice. My father, who loves contributing to his children's dreams, gave me a PC, making the endless revisions technologically painless, and my brother Charles color-coded the plugs so I could figure out how to turn the thing on and taught me how to use it. I can't think of anything my brother Carlton did for this book, but he's a good brother and there was probably something.

There would be no book without the rangers, naturalists, and scientists who generously shared their time and knowledge, including Dr. Bruce Bartholomew, Cassie Burke, Vikki Card, Kevin Cochery, Holly Forbes, Alan Kaplan, Norm Kidder, John Kipping, Ginny Mickelson, Jim Milestone, Al Molina, Mia Monroe, Ray Murphy, Pete Orchard, Bev Ortiz, Dave Pugh, Dan Sealy, Nancy Stone, Alice Tetlow-Noyes, Lanny Waggoner, and Linda Yemoto. Thank you so much. Other equally helpful people undoubtedly should be on this list and are missing solely because I've lost your names. I apologize and thank you also.

Four local experts deserve special thanks. Alice Green taught me about edible seaweeds and reviewed that chapter; Ida Geary taught me about edible land plants and reviewed the entire manuscript. The errors in this book are my own, but there are fewer of them thanks to those two. Dr. Tim McCarthy, of the San Francisco Bay Area Regional Poison Control Center, made time to answer my questions about poisonous plants, giving me the benefit of the PCC's database and local experience; in a subject fraught with tension, his was a calming and very helpful voice. Finally, Neil Havlik, who has been diligently assembling a flora for the East Bay for years, shared his personal wealth of knowledge. Since no flora has yet been published for Alameda or Contra Costa counties, my coverage of the East Bay would have been far more limited if not for his generosity.

It was a lucky day for this book when Rose Craig became involved, back in 1982. She is an avid and observant hiker and knows many of the plants as old friends from Bay Area trails. Dedicated to beauty and accuracy in equal measure, she is passionate about her work as well as her life, this delicate, graceful woman who bicycles 100 miles in a day when the mood strikes her. Thank you, Rose, for giving so much of yourself to this work and for being such a true and steady companion in its completion. And thank you, Bob, for being so gracious when I kept showing up on weekends with more work for her to do.

Malcolm Margolin is a great-hearted coyote in a rabbi disguise, who runs Heyday Books right at that edge where creative freedom, excellence, and chaos stare each other in the face. He edits for honesty. Thanks to his perceptive observations, this book says more of what I meant to say. He understood the spirit of the book from the beginning; helping me free up my voice was the best gift anyone could give me.

He found some more warm-hearted perfectionists to handle copyediting, book design, typesetting, and cover art. I have been so happy talking into the night with Robyn Brode about the evolution of comma usage so that we could reach consensus. It was humbling to see how much flabby verbiage she found to cut and how many stylistic inconsistencies she fixed, and she kept me laughing through the experience. When I wasn't at home with one typeface, Irene Imfeld patiently let me look through all of them until we found another we both could like. She has been generous in taking the time to explain the mysterious world of book design, including such things as preferences in dingbats. She mastered the challenge of integrating Rose's illustrations, in all sizes and shapes, with the text, and she made the book beautiful to our eyes. Rick Heide, copublisher and typesetter, sent back the corrected galleys with his own helpful suggestions, making me feel that even as the type was being set, the book was being read with care and affection and being improved. And Carl Buell thrilled all of us with his painting for the cover. Each of these people made the book his or her own and did much for it.

There are four people who were essential to the creation of this book and I dedicate it to them:

Emma Josephine Kilgore Barkuloo, my great-grandmother, was a loving, rock-steady woman with a great sense of humor, who made her own way in the world on a grammar-school education. She underwrote this endeavor.

My grandmothers both have been psalmists for the wonders of nature, entranced by its details and the philosophy to be found therein. Mary Barkuloo Roos Podea loved philosophy and would quote favorite passages to us in the grand, rolling tones of the Texas Methodist preachers of her childhood. A Quaker, she taught us about creative silence; what made her spirituality so interesting was that she was also a business-woman and a participant in the civil rights and antiwar movements. She nurtured her grandchildren on the idea that we could do anything we set our hearts to, this book included.

Margit Dolenska Friedrich makes the act of writing seem alive and a sensual feast. Her energetic voice, with its haunting trace of Central Europe, makes words sound exotic and beautiful, and she cares passionately about good writing. When we were growing up, she prodded us to use interesting, active verbs at least as often as she told us to stand up straight. Her idea of editing is inviting her grandchildren to cuddle up beside her and be praised for any fresh phrasing she can find in our work. She has spent many weekends on natural history field trips and when we would visit as children, she could identify most of the plants and birds in the mid-Atlantic states.

Richard Roos-Collins husbands my dreams with energy, affection, and resourcefulness. He hiked willingly in the places I needed to explore, not only when it was fun, but also when we yearned to stay home or do something else. He did more than his share of the chores. He made me laugh. He ate all my experiments and fed me fantasies about the book's future. And, with many sighs, he taught me how to take sentences seriously and make them do their work. The evenings we spent reviewing the manuscript count as some of the best times of my life.

Margit Roos-Collins

CONTENTS

CHAPTER 9   TEAS, SEASONINGS, AND MEDICINAL PLANTS   175

PREFACE

What a flood of botanical knowledge we have seen in the last twenty-five years, as tens of thousands of journal articles, monographs, dissertations, reports, conference proceedings, books, and the like have been published. We seem to be gaining knowledge at a monumental rate. Yet I cannot escape the feeling that we have been losing understanding even more rapidly. The loss is not in *what* we know, but in *how* we know. Let me explain.

The Kashaya Pomo, who live in the coastal areas of Sonoma County, as they have for centuries, use acorns for food. They favor the acorns of the tanbark oak above all others, and they call the tree *chishkale,* literally "beautiful tree." *Chishkale.* I wish I could find a way to write this word that would suggest how it really sounds. *Chishkale.* It is spoken with such affection and respect, with a kind of lingering over the word the way one might linger over the name of a lover. *Chishkale,* beautiful tree. It is not just a word, but a prayer, a hymn of praise, as if by uttering the word the speaker was expressing the wonderfulness of a world in which Earthmaker, through His great benevolence, provided this lovely tree for the people who would come. *Chishkale* it is called by people who have had, for so many centuries now, such a passionate understanding of this land of ours.

About six years ago, when I first saw the manuscript for *The Flavors of Home,* I immediately recognized something of that same emotional quality with which my Kashaya friends use the word *chishkale.* Not that the author has presented us with Indian knowledge of the plant world; she hasn't at all. The voice within these pages is that of a thoroughly contemporary woman who moved here from Tennessee and works (of all things) as a lawyer. Perhaps a majority of the plants she describes are likewise recent immigrants, established in the Bay Area only within the last couple of hundred years. Yet her descriptions of collecting berries, nuts, leaves, seaweeds, mushrooms, flowers, and other wild edibles suggest something of the same intimacy, the same depth of affection. Here is the voice of someone in the midst of a serious love affair with the plants around us. It is a curious modern love affair—playful, sensuous, intelligent, and responsible. She sings the ancient hymn of praise with fresh lyrics. What a gift!

Thank you, Margit.

Malcolm Margolin
Berkeley, California

CHAPTER 1

An Introduction to Foraging

The Bay Area may be the most inviting place in the world to explore the flavors of wild plants. Our gentle climate offers a year-round harvest season. Leafy greens and mushrooms flourish in the rainy season, followed by edible blossoms, berries, nuts, and seaweeds in the drier months.

The extraordinarily varied environments found in close proximity here—rocky and sandy seashores, oak and fir and redwood forests, fresh- and salt-water marshes, streambanks, chapparal, mountain tops, and grassy meadows, among others—support an equally extraordinary range of species. Vast tracts of public land surround the Bay, so that all of us live close to a wild place big enough to spare some leaves or berries for tasting. And because the Bay Area is a mecca of environmental education, it is easy to get out and begin tasting plants safely in the company of experienced guides.

What I have treasured most about learning the edible plants of this area has been the feeling of having an intense and private relationship with the land. Observing nature closely can be a grand passion, but tasting moves that relationship beyond the platonic. Plants are the skin of a place, variously rough textured or smooth, aromatic or unscented, sweet or salty. Tasting them has taught me the flavors of the landscape I call home. And each wild mouthful has imprinted itself on my cells. Through the medium of wild plants, the minerals of the places I love have been knit into my bones.

Such intimacy is one of our birthrights. For most of human history, the women and men in every region knew what was edible in their area and when to gather it. Fortunately, learning even a few of the local, edible plants can significantly enrich our connection to a place.

Most of us, as kids, ate at least one wild food. Make-believe games were vastly improved if we could forage for something in the process. When my sister and I picked blackberries or made sassafras tea, we became Laura and Mary Ingalls, at home on the prairie frontier. In Nashville, Tennessee, where I grew up, a type of wild chives grows all year in many lawns, so even in brown winter we had something fresh to nibble. The adults' bane was our pleasure, for try as they might to eradicate them, the chives persisted, and we knew that we could always count on them to flavor our pioneer fantasies.

Once a year, in spring, my mother got into the foraging spirit and gathered polk greens for supper. I disliked all leafy greens except for spinach, but the polk greens' origins in a wild part of our yard made them glamorous enough to be eaten without complaint.

In summer, we chewed sour sorrel in the woods and industriously bit off the tips of hundreds of honeysuckle blossoms because one in ten contained a drop of nectar. Summer was also the time to watch the wild persimmon tree across the road, to see if by any chance it would produce fruit. I remember our astonishment the year it actually bore three to maturity.

All this nibbling was a minor theme in a suburban childhood, and it was taken for granted. One simply didn't walk past a honeysuckle vine without trying at least one of the blossoms, but there was no need to break stride or comment on the action. Chewing chives and tender grass tips on the school grounds was an undiscussed backdrop to our long talks about who loved whom, who hated whom, and whose parents were behaving atrociously.

Growing up and leaving home often marks an end to all that wild-plant tasting. One time my sister got through a low moment in college by making us some acorn bread. Finding the acorns and checking for worm holes satisfied her craving for tangibility, enough so that she could once again face and conquer her physics problems. Otherwise, though, I don't remember any foraging after high school.

As adults, we move to new neighborhoods and rarely think that they, too, must have berry patches and spring greens worth finding. There is enough excitement in choosing our own groceries for a while, and then life gets so busy that simple pleasures like foraging are lost in the rush to make every moment count. If we move to an entirely new climate, the familiar childhood plants don't even appear, making it all the less likely that we will continue to taste wild foods.

That's a shame, because foraging as an adult is very satisfying. Filling a bag with tender leaves of dock, knowing that they are classified as weeds, feels very much like finding that mythical meal, the free lunch. Children are accustomed to being cared for, but for the rest of us, it can be a moving experience to see how much food is provided freely, with no human effort required for cultivation. (Gathering and preparation are a different matter.) With time, you can learn to spot at least half a dozen food plants on almost any hike in the Bay Area. You will find few wild trees and vines covered with large, ripe fruits; this is not the tropics. But you can find acres of green, leafy vegetables and berry bushes, and know the exhilaration of viewing such abundance.

Given our current, and long overdue, preoccupation with humankind's destructive impact on natural balances, I often feel more like an interloper in wild places than a member of the animal tribe. But one day, sitting on a sunny hillside nibbling radish blossoms, I finally understood that I could, even now, go on nibbling indefinitely, grubbing for roots and cracking acorns, and never need another grocery store in my life. Understanding that I still had a place set at the animals' table, and that no particularly human ingenuity, technology, or consciousness was needed in order to be fed, was such sweet relief that it made me cry. How cared for our preagricultural predecessors must have felt (in the good years, at least) living on an earth that kept putting out food for them, day after day after day.

We are dependent now on agriculture because wilderness does not produce enough calories per acre to keep so many of us alive and because we like being able to do other things with our time besides gathering food. Most of us would not willingly take our place at the animals' table again, no matter how glad it makes us to know that it is still there. But as a taster of wild plants, you can nourish that part of yourself that was at home on this planet long before language or farming, so that it can nourish you in return.

The necessarily slow pace of foraging helps us to savor the places where we gather food. As a child, I spent hours just sitting in the woods,

Yerba Santa

daydreaming and observing the wind in the trees. Now, my body is so hungry for exercise after escaping my desk that I spend much of my outdoor time in motion. Walking long and hard is its own joy. But deciding instead to pick enough tender leaves for a salad eases me into a purposeful stillness in which intimacy with a particular place becomes possible. The selection of leaves occupies so little of my mind that the rest is free to dream again and wander over my surroundings. There is time enough for the patterns of sunlight, bird calls, smells, and textures of that unique spot to impress themselves upon me. Through hand, mouth, and eye, a child's intimacy with nature is restored to us while foraging. No wonder adults can become so fond of it.

If you didn't eat any wild plants as a child, it can be a little hard to start as an adult. What if you make a mistake? What if the person teaching you what to eat makes a mistake? In the absence of knowledge, the best way for parents to ensure their children's safety is to inhibit them from eating any wild food. People who have grown up with such inhibitions commonly feel that plant identification is difficult and a matter for experts or eccentrics. Foraging seems a risky business.

Just remember that we are programmed, through millions of years of evolution, to be naturally good at foraging. Anyone who can tell a cabbage from a head of iceberg lettuce can learn to select edible wild plants with confidence.

Sure, the first few times you eat new leaves or berries you may be nervous. When I began trying California plants, I couldn't help being a little surprised at how normal I felt after eating them. But good experiences do chip away at the old fears, and eventually you learn to trust your eyes to choose a plant that's edible and your stomach to digest it.

Foraging Safety and Plant Identification   The bottom line on safety in any pleasurable endeavor is that we want to be able to forget about it and know that it's been taken care of. With foraging, you can take care of safety with one rule: *don't taste a plant unless you can identify it and you know that the species is edible. Don't eat unknowns.*

Learning to identify species is best done with a live guide pointing out live plants, at least in the beginning of a foraging career. Books like this one can tell you what grows in an area, whet your appetite for exploration, and suggest ways to use your harvest. But most potential foragers are not trained to understand and apply botanical terms; and without that training, it is difficult, especially for beginners, to identify plants with certainty from a written description and drawing. I have included the Latin name for each plant so that if you want to read its scientific description, you can easily look it up in a standard reference, such as *A California Flora* by Phillip Munz and David Keck. However, people were successfully recognizing blackberry brambles many millenia before anyone thought to describe them as having "tri-foliate leaves with ovate, dentate leaflets." You can learn to recognize wild berries the same way you learned about peaches; someone shows them to you, you taste them, you pay attention, you see pictures and descriptions of them in books, and gradually you become confident in your knowledge. Wherever you live in the Bay Area, you have opportunities nearby to see edible plants in the flesh, either labeled in a garden or identified by an expert guide. That is how I learned—books were my inspiration, while classes, field trips, and botanical gardens were my sources of plant identification information. After I had learned to identify a plant, books served as useful reminders of its characteristics.

Plant identification field trips are offered by an overwhelming variety of organizations throughout the Bay Area, including university extension programs, community colleges, natural history museums and the California Academy of Sciences, and private nature exploration groups, such as the Point Reyes Field Seminars program. Park rangers also lead such walks free of charge in some of the major parks. For example, the interpretive programs of the East Bay Regional Park District regularly feature edible plant walks and tasting sessions, which you can learn about by calling the district's administrative offices and requesting to be put on the mailing list for their free monthly newsletter.

The East Bay Regional Park Botanical Garden in Tilden Park in Berkeley is devoted entirely to native plants, the great majority of which are clearly labeled. Other gardens with excellent native plant areas are the Strybing Arboretum in Golden Gate Park in San Francisco and the U.C. Berkeley Botanical Garden in Strawberry Canyon in Berkeley.

Since most of the edible berries and nuts are natives, botanical gardens are excellent places to learn to recognize them (but not, of course, to pick them). Wild greens, though, are generally non-native. Classified as weeds, they are removed from gardens and are ignored by many guides unless an outing is focused on edibles. If you want to learn them, tell your teacher so that she or he will point them out to you.

When you are shown a plant, look up its description and drawing or photograph in this or other guidebooks. Try to match the real plant's features to the book's version. That will make you sensitive to details in the plant's construction, so that you can recognize the species in other settings.

Note that being a relative of an edible plant is not good enough. Some-one very dear to me almost tasted the roots of a plant because it looked related to the wild carrot she knew from back East. She kept going, instead, thanks to some inner whisper of caution and a desire not to be late for our hike together. The plant was indeed in the carrot family, but it was poison hemlock. An experimental chew could have landed her in intensive care. Similarly, tomatoes and potatoes are in the same family as the deadly nightshade (which is why Europeans were afraid to eat tomatoes for more than a century after explorers brought them back from the Americas). Fortunately, most plants don't look like their relatives any more than people look like their siblings; you can see the relation-ship, but they're easy to tell apart. Just don't assume that all members of a family will be equally good.

In Chapter 2, some of the most common or important poisonous plants are discussed. If you are aware of them, and if you taste only plants that you have identified specifically as edible, your chances of making a serious mistake will be close to zero.

When you know you have found an edible plant, bear in mind a few more precautions. One is that the berries of a plant can be poisonous even if the leaves are edible, and vice versa. Or the mature leaves may be poisonous while the immature ones are a delicacy. So only eat those parts of a plant that are specifically described as edible.

Second, there is always the small chance that a wild plant, like any new food, will give you an allergic reaction. It's smart not to eat a lot of it the first time. If it agrees with you, as it almost certainly will, you can eat it with abandon the next time.

A final point to remember is that the plants along roads are exposed to auto exhaust and sometimes chemical sprays. Lead emissions from leaded gasoline concentrate in the leaves of roadside plants. Leave at least 15 feet between roads and your gathering places; 25 to 50 feet is even better. Wild edibles in city parks, farm fields, or orchards may have been doused with herbicides or pesticides, so if you gather from such places, wash the foods well.

To sum up, the rules for safety are these:

- *Avoid roadside foraging and be alert to the possibility of chemical sprays elsewhere.*
- *Eat only a small amount of a wild food the first time you try it.*
- *Eat only those portions of a plant which you know to be edible.*
- *Learn to identify the most poisonous wild plants so that you never taste them by mistake.*
- *And, most importantly, only taste a plant if you know from a reliable source that it is an edible species.*

If you follow these guidelines, your foraging should be entirely pleasant, undisturbed by anxiety.

The Ethics and Practicalities of Bay Area Foraging   With over six million potential foragers living in or visiting this area, we have to use some common sense. This is a book about the joys of tasting nature, not of devouring it.

Happily, many species can absorb our attentions with great resilience. Weeds spring to mind. Many familiar weeds are edible, tasty, and full of vitamins. In some cases, they were the original species from which we domesticated our vegetables. Others are garden escapes that have naturalized. Most of them will surprise you with the familiarity of their flavors.

And we will always have enough of them. Weeds are the plant world's toughest characters. They thrive in earth so poor that little else can grow. Where the soil is compacted by feet or car tires, or where it has been recently burnt or scalped, weeds are often the only plants to be found. Their chief and critical value in the scheme of things is to protect the soil from blowing away and to trap rain water in otherwise barren places. With time, they add enough humus to the soil so that it can support more demanding, slow-growing species.

Weeds have a way of turning up where they aren't needed and causing trouble, however. Great world travelers, their seeds hitch rides on cargo and animals and come to rest in soils far from their natural competitors and diseases. Their hardiness, their resistance to cold, heat, and drought, and their superabundant seed production combine to make them strong rivals of the species native to an area. For example, the Bay Area's hills are covered with introduced grassy weeds that came on the hides of cattle. The native bunch grasses that once reigned here have been pushed back to a few tiny areas.

When you pick a weed to eat, you simply give the native plants more breathing room. Therefore, dozens of introduced species are included here, with recipes for their leaves, stalks, seeds, and flowers. Eat all the wild mustard greens you wish, and our fields and vineyards will still be yellow next spring. Developing familiarity with edible weeds has another advantage: you can find the same species in many other parts of the United States, whereas Bay Area natives often grow in more circumscribed areas.

Several classes of native plants can also feed us without harm to themselves, and so are included here. As long as we leave some of the harvest for the animals that depend on it, we can pick wild berries and nuts in most places to our heart's content. The native trees and bushes that provide teas and seasonings can spare a few leaves without damage. (It is unnecessary and wrong to break off whole branches, as past generations

California Bay

once did; the raw place left in the wood provides easy access for parasites and infections.) Mushrooms can be picked for personal use with a clear conscience because the part above ground is like a berry; the critical part of the mushroom plant is the network of white threads just below the surface of the soil. Seaweeds are plentiful on this coast, and proper harvesting techniques can preserve this resource while we explore their culinary contributions. Finally, some native greens, like miner's lettuce, are so abundant and such a part of traditional Bay Area foraging that you will find them in this book as well.

I have omitted some edible species that the local Indians once enjoyed. The roots and seeds of certain wildflowers and the delicate leaves of some native greens are too vulnerable to depletion, now that our numbers have swelled. Besides, we can never have enough wildflowers in our meadows; their blossoms are more precious than their food value. Our laws reflect this need for protection, so that on most public land, at least, foraging for the omitted species would not be legal anyway.

Besides deciding what to pick, the other big question relating to conscience and law is where to pick. Virtually every park or public property is protected by laws prohibiting the disturbance of plants found in it. The laws were passed originally to protect against people who came to public lands with a profit motive and gathered commercial quantities of plant matter. They also were designed to stop people from picking wildflowers and removing or destroying native plants.

Many of the same parks and public lands, however, also have policies or regulations allowing people to collect berries, nuts, and limited quantities of seaweeds for their own use. The land managers are sympathetic to the widespread human craving for a chance to touch and taste nature directly, so long as the level of use does not threaten the plants or the animals that depend on them. If you are unsure of a park's policies, ask a ranger or park naturalist about the species you want to taste. My experience has been that if a species is common enough, you will usually get permission to try it. If you want to pick wild greens of an introduced weed species, the activity may even be welcomed. However, careless or greedy foragers could wind up with a steep bill for their afternoon in the park!

For most of the edible plants in this book, I have mentioned parks where they grow. This was done to give you an idea of their range and of the environment they need. *A park's inclusion in this book does not mean that it is okay to pick the leaves or berries there. The only way you can find the answer to that question is to ask a naturalist or ranger at that park.*

Some parks are clearly more suited to plant tasting than others. In general, the rule is: the larger and emptier the park, the better, since the vegetation will be under less pressure from visitors. Muir Woods, with its busloads of tourists, is the classic example of a bad place to pick things; the forest survives only because visitors respect its vulnerability.

Tilden Park above Berkeley is another example of a park so popular that it would not be fair to forage there. This is especially true because the rangers at the Nature Center offer free edible-plant walks occasionally, and perform the invaluable service of showing people how to identify the plants and how to use them. The only reason they can do this is that most people live up to their end of the deal and use their new knowledge in less trodden areas. There is enough land in the Bay Area to support a lot of wild-plant tasters, if we choose our species and places with care.

Foraging on public land does raise one question for which there is no simple answer. When you are happily gathering a few common, edible seaweeds, well within the collection limit for that particular beach, what do you do when parents, seeing you, begin to collect tidepool creatures for their child's amusement, ignorant of the regulations prohibiting such behavior? And what about those who see you taking mushrooms and conclude, wrongly, that it is open season on picking wildflowers? I don't know how often this happens in fact, but it is a concern that park rangers and foragers live with.

Be conscious of the problem. Collecting in remote areas minimizes the risk of misinterpretation by others; plus, solitude outdoors is delicious, as long as safety is not an issue. Be prepared to speak up, gently and with humor, if possible, if you see people engaged in a type of collecting that is harmful. We all have a lot to learn about the stewardship of our environment; you are most likely to be heard and heeded if your tone reflects that reality.

You will probably find that if you already like a place and then begin tasting the plants that grow there, your sense of connection to that place will deepen powerfully. Since our species almost always puts its own needs first, our capacity and need to connect to the land with all of our senses is one of the best defenses nature has. May this book fan the embers of your own need and show you some new ways to experience that connection.

Finding the Plants   At the end of each plant description, you will find a section titled *Where and When to Find It.* Here are a few pointers about how to use and interpret these sections.

Any plant will reach the harvesting stage sooner in a sunny location than in a shady one. The harvest times given, which may be several months or longer, are meant to cover all the locations in which the species grows. You will find that a specific plant has a much shorter season.

For example, chickweed can be found ready to eat in one place or another from October through May, or longer. But the particular chickweed in my neighbor's yard is only available through January. After that, it is crowded out by sow thistle and other plants. So, use the time periods in this book to learn when to look for a plant, but realize that the particular plants you find will be ready to harvest for only a portion of those time periods.

What's more, shifts in the rain patterns affect the harvest times. In a wet year, chickweed is lush by October, but during a drought, you may not find enough to make a salad until late November. One of the great satisfactions of foraging is developing a sense for the normal rhythm of a year in the plant community. With time, you will gain an intuitive feel for the timing of the Bay Area's wild harvests. You will learn that if miner's lettuce is available unusually late in the spring, then you'll have to wait a bit longer than average for cattail pollen and edible seaweeds, because the rain that prolongs the one slows the others. A rule of thumb: since it is the ends of a harvest period, rather than the middle, that are affected by changing weather patterns, the surest time to look for a plant is in the middle of the time period given.

The descriptions of where to find each species come from three sources: my own records, interviews with botanists and park rangers, and published floras. Floras are books describing all the plants that grow in a region. They explain how common or rare a species is and what habitats it requires, and list, in a general way, some of the places where a species has been found. Floras are themselves compilations of the author's own records and the records of other botanists, sometimes going back a hundred years or more.

As you can imagine, a shrub that was found in Sausalito fifty years ago may not be there anymore. The little gully that nurtured it may have long since been filled in for housing. However, knowing that the shrub has been found there is still useful information. It tells you that that species is likely to be found elsewhere on hilly slopes bordering the Bay.

Do not expect to find plants for the first time on the basis of the general listings in the *Where and When to Find It* sections. However, once you have learned to recognize a species, the listings of locations and habitats can be very useful to you. If you learn, for example, that a plant is rare along the coast but common in the Berkeley/Hayward hills, it's clear where to concentrate your efforts at finding it. The descriptions of habitats will help you build an accurate set of expectations about plants you are likely to find in a given setting. In dry chapparal, you will learn to look for yerba santa, coyote mint, and sagebrush, but will waste no time scanning the trailsides for nasturtium, which needs cool moisture.

Certain place names come up again and again, whereas others are completely ignored. This is because floras cover some areas more thoroughly than others. You will find all species growing in many more places than those listed here. The lists are only starting points; your own explorations will lead you to far more harvesting sites than any book could include. A list of the Bay Area floras and a selection of other books about foraging and plant identification are included at the back of the book.

CHAPTER 2

Poisonous Plants

T he safe way to eat wild plants is to choose only those which you know to be safe. ✿ *Don't ever taste a plant unless you can identify it and know that it is an edible species.* ✿ A few common garden plants and houseplants are deadly poisonous, such as oleander and rhododendron. Others can cause distress of one kind or another. So the greenery in your home and yard is no exception to this rule. If you forage with your children, it is essential that they understand the existence of poisonous plants. School-age children can become competent to recognize many edible species independently, and children who can weave wild foods into their make-believe games love to do so. But before you introduce your kids to this whole, rich experience, be sure they have developed enough common sense to leave unknown plants uneaten. ✿ Having said all this, it should be superfluous to include a list of some poisonous plants. However, certain ones are so tempting or common or deadly that it's worth a forager's while to become familiar with them, so they are described below. In particular, I urge you to become familiar with poison oak and poison hemlock as soon as possible. This chapter is not a complete list of the poisonous species that grow in the Bay Area. For a relatively comprehensive treatment, try *Poisonous Plants of California* by Thomas C. Fuller and Elizabeth McClintock (Berkeley: University of California Press, 1986).

California Buckeye *(Aesculus californica)*

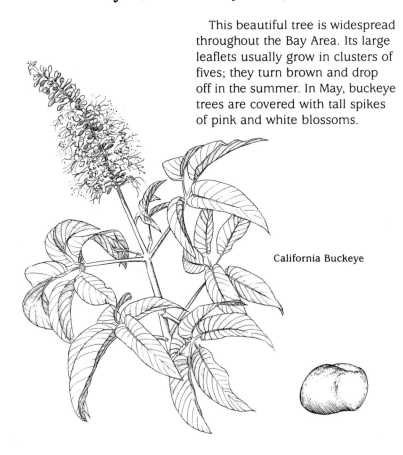

This beautiful tree is widespread throughout the Bay Area. Its large leaflets usually grow in clusters of fives; they turn brown and drop off in the summer. In May, buckeye trees are covered with tall spikes of pink and white blossoms.

California Buckeye

The nuts that follow them are polished to a high luster with a chestnut brown exterior, and are unparalleled as objects to rub in one's hand. One of the most endearing sights on a January walk is a buckeye nut, lying by the path, sprouting a healthy, infant tree, complete with a set or two of perfect leaflets. These nuts were eaten by the Indians as emergency food, but only after extensive leaching made them safe. Eaten plain, they are bitter and quite poisonous.

Baneberry *(Actaea* species*)*

In late summer, these plants produce shiny red or white berries that are poisonous and are clustered at the end of long, bare stems. You may see them occasionally on moist, wooded slopes in Marin, the Peninsula, and the Oakland/Berkeley hills.

Baneberry

Water Hemlock *(Cicuta* species*)*

Water hemlock and poison hemlock are two of the three most poisonous plants found in North America (the third, water parsnip or *Sium suave,* does not grow in the Bay Area). Both hemlocks are neurotoxins, so they shut down a person's internal communication network.

Water hemlock has mottled purple blotches and spots on its main stems, and where the branches leave the stem they are wrapped in noticeable sheathes. The flowers are white.

This plant is found occasionally in Marin and on the Peninsula, and is quite uncommon, but present, in the East Bay. It grows in marshy areas or around springs.

Water Hemlock

Poison Hemlock *(Conium maculatum)*

This hemlock looks feathery and pretty, at least in the spring, and it grows as a weed all over the place. You will find it throughout the Bay Area wherever there is a moderate amount of human disturbance, such as along roads and trailsides. This is the plant that was used to kill Socrates.

Poison hemlock foliage changes its appearance as the plant matures. The young plants, up to a couple of feet high, have lush, ferny leaves that look somewhat like parsley or carrot tops, only bigger. In late spring and summer, as the plants develop a central stalk and flowerheads, the leaves become wispy and lacy. Eventually, the mature plants can grow up to 12 feet tall, although 3 to 6 feet is the norm. By mid-summer, most develop a bedraggled, lanky, weedy look.

Poison Hemlock

To identify hemlock, look for the purple blotching at the base of the main stems and the white flowers. A little drama helps me remember things, so I think of the purplish red spots as being the blood of hemlock's victims.

Fortunately, those victims are rare, at least in this area. Because most foragers know this plant, the Bay Area's Poison Control Center has had only two cases of exposure to deal with in the last ten years. The doctors cleared as much of the hemlock as possible from the patients' digestive tracts and both survived.

In winter, the tiny plants, 1 to 4 inches high, can be a bother in otherwise excellent patches of chickweed or other greens. Rather than risk picking it by mistake, I avoid harvesting edible plants in hemlock-infested spots. Another way you can eat hemlock by mistake is to chew some of its seeds when you think you are harvesting fennel seeds. The two plants don't look that much alike, but I once saw them growing intermingled so that their seeds were almost indistinguishable. If you bite into a supposed fennel seed and don't taste licorice or anise, play it safe and spit it out. It's probably just a flavorless fennel, so don't get scared, but do spit.

Poison Hemlock

Silktassel Bush *(Garrya elliptica* or *G. fremontii)*

Silktassel is known for its tassels of blossoms, which open in mid-winter when flowers are most appreciated. The leaves are leathery and evergreen. Its thick, long clusters of berries are poisonous. Depending on the species, the berries are either black or purple and are relatively hairless or covered with fine, silky hairs.

Silktassel Bush

Lupine *(Lupinus* species*)*

All lupines produce seeds in tempting-looking pods. They look so much like pea pods that you should be sure your children know that lupine pods and seeds are quite poisonous. The same holds true for most other pea-pod-producing plants, including wisteria and broom (an invader that is taking over whole hillsides). Even garden peas are said to be poisonous if eaten in enormous quantities; in the case of their wild relatives, a relatively small amount can cause permanent damage, especially in a child.

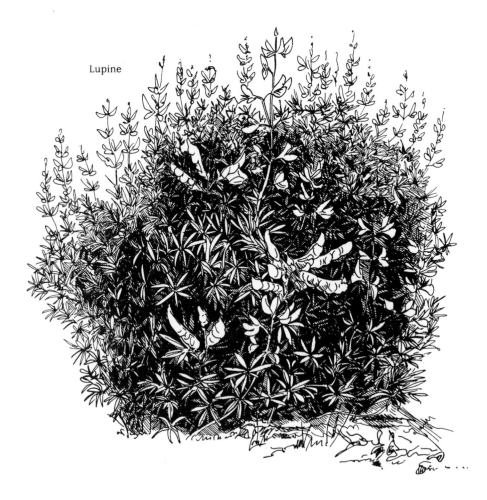

Lupine

Wild Cucumber *(Marah oreganus)*

The wild cucumber fruits contain a poison called cucurbitacin, and at least one person has died from eating them. I've heard that extensive leaching can render the fruits safe, but why take the risk? The plant is most easily recognized by its curly tendrils, which form almost perfect cones that reach out for the nearest support. It is fairly widespread, growing in coastal canyons and on wooded hillsides.

Wild
Cucumber

Poison Oak *(Rhus diversiloba)*

This is unfortunately one of the most common shrubs in the Bay Area, in part because it can adapt itself to a wide variety of habitats. In deep woods, poison oak becomes a vine, though "vine" hardly describes the way it fans out massively from the trunks of supporting trees. On windswept hills, it grows low to the ground, while in sunny, protected locations, it can mature into a handsome, rounded shrub, taller than the hikers who carefully avoid it. In all its forms, this species has the same glossy, lobed leaves in groups of three. Learning to recognize them should be a first priority for anyone who wants to explore the outdoors in this area.

People vary in their sensitivity to poison oak, but skin contact with the leaves, twigs, or berries will cause many to break out in a rash. The rash can be itchy, painful, swollen, and otherwise unpleasant. Needless to say, swallowing the white berries causes very serious swelling of the throat. Even if you seem immune to the rash, it is wise to avoid the plant to lessen the chance of developing a sensitivity to it later on. Because poison oak is so prevalent, long pants are a good idea on any hikes away from major, well-cleared trails. It's enough of a bother just to make sure that your arms don't brush against the stuff without having to worry about your legs, as well.

One thing can be said in defense of this plant. It does provide much of the best autumn color we have. Beginning in July, the leaves turn deep red, and because they are so shiny, the effect is quite striking, especially against the straw-colored grass. Look, but don't touch!

Poison
Oak

Black Nightshade *(Solanum nodiflorum)*
Blue Witch *(S. umbelliferum)*

Fortunately, the deadly night-shade, also known as belladonna, does not grow here; but plenty of its toxic or questionable relatives do. Most of the plants are low, weedy shrubs, although in the case of blue witch, the flowers are quite attractive. Other *solanum* blossoms look quite similar to those of the related tomato. Night-shade and blue witch fruits are attached to the plant by a distinc-tive, four-pointed cap. Don't eat any part of these plants.

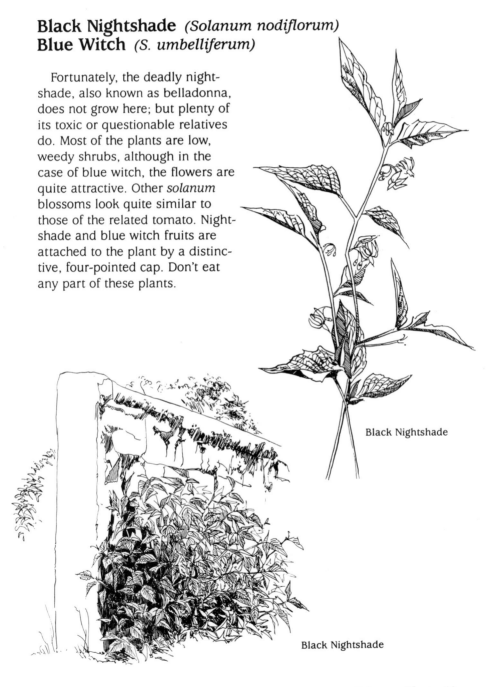

Black Nightshade

Black Nightshade

California Nutmeg *(Torreya californica)*

This is a tree of the north coast; Howell *(Marin Flora)* noted it in "deep, well-watered canyons" and north-facing slopes. A member of the yew family, it grows into a stately conifer with very sharp needles. The smooth, greenish fruits (the "nutmegs") are streaked with purple and are considered poisonous, despite the name.

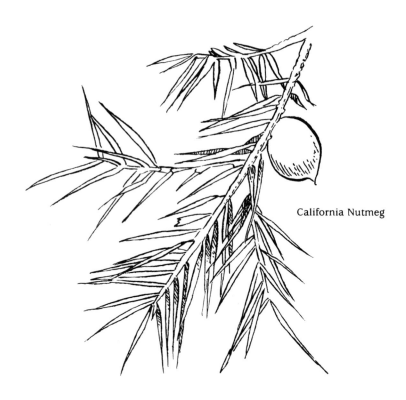

California Nutmeg

Please note that the berries of red elderberry (discussed on p. 60), asparagus (p. 100), and mistletoe are also poisonous. And remember, the basic rule is: *don't put something in your mouth if you don't know for sure that it is edible.*

CHAPTER 3

Edible Blossoms

I think native wildflowers generally ought to be left in peace, but introduced species don't arouse any of the same protective instincts in me. After all, just by coming here and thriving, they have demonstrated their ability to cope with human disruption and, in some cases, to need it. ✿ So, I've felt free to discover the pleasures of eating five types of flowers—mustard, radish, nasturtium, onion, and oxalis—each of which came here from elsewhere and is in no danger of being harmed by our attentions. Surprisingly, they don't taste flowery the way rose petals do. They taste like radishes, broccoli, onions, or lemons and fit more naturally in a salad than a dessert. ✿ Each of the following species is in bloom in April and May. For special occasions, it's glorious to make a salad with all of them at once— orange, white, yellow, pink, and purple amid the lettuce. At a spring wedding, for example, what food could better celebrate the beginning of a family than a feast of flowers, which are themselves the source of new generations?

Wild Radish *(Raphanus sativas)*
Common or Field Mustard *(Brassica campestris)*
Charlock *(B. kaber,* also *B. arvensis)*
Mediterranean or Summer Mustard *(B. geniculata)*
Black Mustard *(B. nigra)*

Wild Radish

I have nothing but affection for these members of the Mustard family. Foraging for them is pure pleasure. Few paths are more inviting than those which lead through waist-high fields of blooming mustard or radish. When I am introducing friends to edible wild plants, these two are frequently the ones with which we begin. Even if they never eat another wild mouthful in their lives, they remember their first bites fondly.

Radish and all the local mustards belong to the Mustard family or *Cruciferae.* The family contains an unusually wide variety of edible, cultivated species: broccoli, Brussels sprouts, cabbage, cauliflower, horseradish, kohlrabi, rutabaga, and turnips, among them. The radish species that grows wild here is the same species as the domesticated radish, which is just bred to have a larger root. It was eaten in Egypt even before the Pyramids were built and has been raised in China and Japan for at least as long. Most of our wild mustards are also grown as crops for their seeds or leaves. The Latin name, *Cruciferae,* comes from the shape of the blossoms: four petals arranged like a cross or crucifix.

The blossoms are my favorite part. Though the skies are cool with rain and deciduous trees are still bare, mustard is in its fullest bloom in March, coloring vast fields and orchards pure yellow. Our blooming season begins subtly, with scattered harbingers like the snowy plums, but mustards announce the season's arrival to whole valleys at a time.

There's a story about the introduction of mustard to California that botany writers keep passing on without being able to confirm it. It is fact that the mustards and radish are native to Europe. And we know that black mustard arrived in California sometime during the Spanish Mission period between 1769 and 1824, because its seeds have been found in adobe building bricks from that period. It is legend that the Spanish padres spread black mustard between the southern missions and San Francisco to keep them-selves from getting lost. The idea is that they dropped seeds along the way as they explored north-ward, counting on the seeds to produce a trail of yellow flowers that they could follow home in the spring. At least one respected botanist disputes this tale, saying that the padres simply followed well-worn Indian trails. But I think writers will keep passing the story on as long as possible, because we love so much to imagine it.

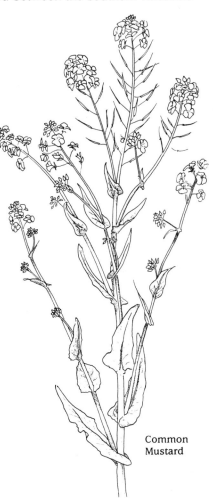

Common Mustard

Field mustard, radish, and char-lock were here by the time the '49ers arrived, so that wave of eastern migrants never knew a California without its fields of yel-low in March. Summer mustard came much later than the others and wasn't observed in the Bay Area until 1915.

Radish blossoms also appear in March, with a pastel prettiness that lasts into the summer. Each plant produces flowers that are predominantly white, pink, purple, or occasionally, yellow. The colors are all mixed together in thickly blooming, sweet-smelling patches.

Try sitting a while in such a radish patch, head deep in flowers, on a warm April day. Give yourself up to that pastel ocean until it seems utterly natural to be there. If part of you is Ferdinand the bull, this is your chance to wallow in flowers until you are buzzy and light headed with contentment. My Ferdinand self has been happier in radish patches than anywhere else I have been.

Much of the fun in all this flower appreciation comes from eating the blossoms and privately savoring their down-to-earth, unflowery flavors. Mustard buds and blossoms taste just like raw broccoli heads. And those sweetly pink radish flowers have a decidedly radishy bite that warms the mouth and makes them doubly irresistible. Try sprinkling a handful on a vegetable dip. What a joy it is each time we find something (or someone) with a combination of positive traits that cuts across the usual expectations. Radish blossoms have that refreshing quality, with a look and fragrance that's ultrafeminine and a taste that's salt of the earth.

The plump, wild radish seedpods are good raw in salads, to be consumed by true radish lovers; they pack enough of a punch that I wouldn't recommend them except to people who voluntarily eat cultivated radishes. Mustard seedpods are long and thin and lined with the proverbially tiny seeds. Black mustard seeds are the ones traditionally

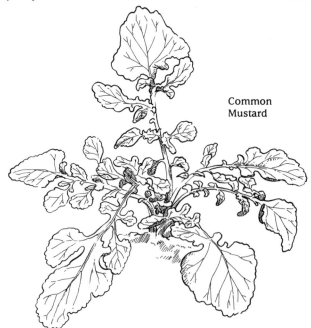

Common
Mustard

used for mustard, though the others can be substituted. The Romans crushed and mixed them with a little new wine as a condiment; later cultures used vinegar as the binder.

When fully ripe, the seedpods split open. If you want to make mustard from the wild seeds, you need to gather the pods just before they split. I have not done this, but the recommended way is to gather the still-closed, upper pods from plants whose lower pods have already opened.

Dry the pods on a clean surface for several days, then flail them to break them open and release the seeds. The dry seeds can be ground in a blender to make powdered mustard. Mixing ¼ cup of the powder with 2 or 3 tablespoons of water, vinegar, or beer will produce a very hot, Chinese-style mustard sauce. To make the milder American style, follow the recipe in any basic cookbook, such as *Joy of Cooking.*

Radish and mustard leaves are among the first greens to appear after the rains begin. Along with miner's lettuce, dock, and chickweed, they are my favorite wild greens—abundant, tender, tasty, and easy to harvest. It is likely that the mustard varieties vary somewhat in their flavor, but I haven't paid attention to which ones I was eating, so can only tell you that all the mustard greens I have tried have tasted at least okay and usually quite good. One book mentions that charlock leaves are particularly tasty, but that's the least common mustard in this area. I generally prefer radish to mustard greens, so if you don't like mustard greens, be sure to give radish leaves a chance to please you.

By November (October in rainy years), you can go to mustard and radish areas and find a thick covering of healthy new leaves, about a foot high. The young leaves can feel rough, almost prickly, but that quality disappears with even brief cooking.

Both types of leaves are large and irregularly lobed. The flavor is better in winter, before the plants flower, although I have eaten and enjoyed them after flowering began.

Raw, the leaves are slightly peppery and can be good in salads if they are chopped coarsely. Steamed until tender, they become milder in flavor. Radish leaves lose their radish taste completely. Mustard greens keep a trace of bitterness, but it is not objectionable. Both greens taste best with a squeeze of lemon or a splash of vinegar.

I like to make a simple, crustless quiche with these leaves. It is good hot or cold, and makes a fine light meal or picnic food. You can use wild radish and mustard leaves in any of the ways you would use the stronger-tasting grocery-store greens, such as cultivated mustard or kale. Like their domesticated peers, they are loaded with Vitamin A.

RADISH OR MUSTARD PIE

- 1 onion
- 4 to 6 cups radish or mustard leaves
- 1 cup grated sharp cheddar
- 1 cup grated mozarella
- 2 eggs
- nutmeg, salt, pepper, and Worcestershire sauce

Chop the onion and saute it in a little oil until tender. Rinse the radish or mustard leaves (or a combination of the two) and chop coarsely.

Add the leaves to the onion and stir them over low to medium heat until the leaves have wilted. Whisk the eggs until lightly beaten.

Then, in a 9-inch pie pan, cake pan, or ovenproof frying pan, combine the onions and greens, the grated cheeses, and the eggs. Add nutmeg, salt, pepper, and Worcestershire sauce, all to taste. A thin layer of grated cheddar sprinkled over the surface gives the pie an especially pleasing color.

Bake the pie at 375° F. for about 30 minutes or until the top begins to brown. Slice it and eat.

Where and When to Find Them   Finding mustard in bloom is no problem in any Bay Area county, for it is common to abundant and widespread throughout the area in disturbed or cultivated ground. The great displays tend to be in agricultural areas, although not always. At Ft. Cronkhite in Marin County, the hidden oceanside vale (toward San Francisco from the main valley) is solid yellow in March. The farming region of Brentwood and Byron in the East Bay is good, but my favorite mustard displays are those along Route 1, near Half Moon Bay. The vast, bright fields are framed between the Coast Range and the Pacific in what must surely be one of the most beautiful agricultural settings in America.

The spring-blooming mustard species that colors these vast areas, common mustard, begins flowering in February and is at full strength in March. Black mustard does most of its blooming between March and May. Summer mustard flowers primarily in the summer (did you guess?), although you will see it along trails and roads and in vacant places from spring through early fall.

Radish is common to abundant in Marin and on the Peninsula. In the East Bay, you will find more of it in the area of Chabot and Tilden parks than further inland. Two beautiful radish patches are at Lands End in Lincoln Park in San Francisco and at the end of Pierce Point Road on the Point Reyes peninsula. Both places have enough of the flowers to sweeten the air. But other fine radish displays probably grow within a few miles of you, wherever you live in the Bay Area.

Radish blooms from March through October, depending on the location, but in most areas, April and May are its peak months. The big Pierce Point Road patch is at its best in May and turns brown by June, but nearby, radishes bloom all along the path to the beach much later in the summer.

The seedpods of both species appear soon after the plants begin to flower and continue to be available for months. The leaves are at their best from October or November until the end of February, and are most abundant in January and February.

Oxalis, Sour Grass, or Bermuda Buttercup
(Oxalis pes-caprae)

This cloverlike plant from South Africa and its many relatives are well known to children, who chew on the sour leaves, flowers, and stems. I still remember the day when a grade-school classmate taught me to recognize it in the woods. When my husband was tutoring a child from a very poor, densely populated section of Oakland, they walked past some sour grass growing in a vacant lot and the child said that it was good to eat. When I led a group of sophisticated, privileged San Francisco children on an edible-plant walk, the sour grass needed no introduction: they ran to it. Across generations and economic lines, across the continent, children apparently keep passing down this one piece of foraging lore. The tradition is sweet to see; it doesn't fit the usual images of modern childhood.

Just in case you missed out on this piece of your education, sour grass has leaflets grouped in threes. Each leaflet is heart shaped and creased down the middle. At night and during cold days, the leaves fold down like a closed umbrella. The five-petaled flowers stand atop long, thin stems and are a clear lemon yellow.

All parts of the plant are edible and are sour due to high levels of

Oxalis

oxalic acid. The leaves and flowers are attractive, tender, and tasty in salads. The yellow flowers look especially appealing in a salad of dark green spinach leaves. Their sour but delicate flavor makes them an ideal garnish for any dish, such as fish or fruit salads, on which you might squeeze fresh lemon or use a tart dressing. The leaves stay tender and tart when cooked; try combining them with other greens. Eating great quantities can give people a stomach ache similar to eating too many green apples, but this is rarely a problem.

Note: Despite the name Bermuda buttercup, this plant is not the same as those *Ranunculus* species commonly called buttercups. Buttercups have waxy petals, very different leaves, and are toxic.

Where and When to Find It   If you have kids, ask them. Otherwise, watch for oxalis in orchards, fields, gardens, and yards. This weed thrives on rich soil, so it's often found in the neglected corners of urban parks; I have seen large clumps of it in the Presidio, in Mt. Lake Park, and in Lincoln Park, all in San Francisco. Sour grass is widespread in the East Bay and southern Marin, and is especially common along the Peninsula coast.

The leaves can be eaten year round. The flowers usually bloom from February through July, with some mavericks continuing longer or beginning earlier.

Nasturtium *(Tropaeolum majus)*

Nasturtium is a garden plant of Peruvian origin that has naturalized (gone wild) here. It grows in dense masses along the coast, climbing on trees and covering moist hillsides. Once introduced into a fog-zone garden, it will hold its own indefinitely and needs no care.

The leaves are rounded, with a starburst pattern of veins radiating from the center. The flowers are stunning: large and boldly orange, they provide one of the more exotic spectacles in the local flora.

The flowers and leaves both are so respectable as foodstuffs that they are included in *Joy of Cooking*. Nasturtium is easy to identify and doesn't look like any other Bay Area plant. As a salad ornament, no supermarket item can compare with nasturtium blossoms for beauty and dramatic impact.

The only reason to avoid nasturtium would be a dislike of radishes. Nasturtium is in that large class of wild edibles with a distinctly radishy taste when eaten raw. When you first chew a leaf, it will have a mild, green taste that's pleasant enough. But after a moment, your mouth will heat up with the potent radishy bite. You can imagine how attractive the leaves are in salads, given their unusual, circular shape and wheel-spoke pattern of veins. Just be sure to mix them with plenty of milder greens.

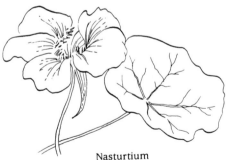

Nasturtium

Adding a layer of the flowers to the top of a salad is a true showstopper. Nothing in most people's culinary background has prepared them for dining on large, exquisite blossoms. Give it a try. Your guests will remember the meal long afterward.

The flowers also have a bite. If you don't like hot foods, you can still enjoy the petals, which are relatively mild. The heat is concentrated in the center of each flower.

Another approach is to stuff the blossoms. For example, chicken or seafood salads, or cottage and cream cheese blended with fruits or tomatoes all work well. Served with crusty bread, stuffed nasturtium blossoms on a bed of salad greens make a lunch that's exciting for both the eyes and the tastebuds.

The leaves are also good as a cooked green. There is no noticeable difference in flavor or texture between young and mature leaves. Unlike some wild greens that become meltingly tender with cooking, nasturtium leaves retain a definite texture, much like spinach. So, depending on whether you prefer chopped or leaf spinach, treat nasturtium leaves accordingly.

I steam them for 5 minutes. Heat removes all radishy taste and there's no bitterness in them. The leaves develop an intriguing sweetness in that brief cooking, and make one of the better wild greens. Overcooking doesn't

Nasturtium

change the flavor much, but it can release a strong aroma similar to that of overcooked cabbage or Brussels sprouts.

Another use for nasturtiums is to pickle the seedpods, which can then be substituted for capers. Collect the pods as soon as the flower petals drop off, and make the pickles as soon as possible afterward. *Joy of Cooking* contains a recipe for this delicacy.

Where and When to Find It   In this climate, nasturtium keeps some leaves all year, although they are lusher in spring and summer than in winter. The flowers begin to appear in April, become abundant by May, and continue to bloom until November.

This species needs moisture. It is reported to grow in Palo Alto, along the banks of Temescal Creek in Oakland, and on San Bruno Mountain. But the classic situation for it is along the coast. I have seen large mats of nasturtium covering the ground on Mt. Davidson and in Lincoln Park in San Francisco, and along Route 1 in Stinson Beach.

One of the most spectacular displays is in the woods above the ranger station at Ft. Point in San Francisco. Go there sometime in May. Under heavy shade, a wild and otherworldly garden flourishes. Masses of white calla lilies bloom amidst an entire hillside of orange nasturtium, so close to the Bay that you can hear the waves breaking on the sand.

Wild Onion *(Allium triquetrum)*

A number of *Allium* species grow here, but most are native. *Allium triquetrum* came from Europe and Asia. Even though its white flowers are delicate and attractive, it can be an unwanted volunteer in gardens. It thrives in our fog-zone neighborhood, and I saw a gardener's pick-up truck piled high with the rejects from one yard alone.

This onion tastes far milder than commercial scallions. It has no bite, even when raw. But both the stalks and flowers smell and taste oniony and are good in salads. Try sprinkling the blossoms over the surface of a vegetable dip. Most people are tickled to scoop up a pretty, edible flower on the tip of a carrot stick. The stem is tough and stringy where it joins the flower, so don't leave any of it attached to the blossoms you use.

Where and When to Find It

This wild onion is becoming naturalized in San Francisco and in
towns in Marin and the East Bay.
Look for it in shady, moist places.

The plant blooms in March,
April, and May.

See Also

Elderberry Blossoms, page 60
Clover Blossoms, page 198

Wild Onion

CHAPTER 4

Berries

When you are attracted to the bright red or shiny blue of a berry, and taste it, and like it so much that you eat a lot of them, you are doing exactly what the plant "wants." The ecological purpose of a berry is to tempt. Birds and mammals like ourselves are supposed to eat them, as well as the seeds they contain, and then help disperse the seeds by depositing them at some later time in a little pile of fertilizer. ✿ The tiny seeds contain within them all the nourishment that the embryonic huckleberry bush or blackberry vine will need to sprout. The berry flesh surrounding them is, from the seeds' perspective, not food but purely cosmetic packaging designed to lure us into taking them where they want to go. ✿ Not all berry species attract all animal species. Berries that would poison us are popular with other mammals; possibly the ones we enjoy are poisonous to some animals, too. Fortunately, there are more than a dozen reasonably common, tasty berry species in this area designed to attract humans as seed dispersers. I have had a good time discovering which ones are my favorites; I hope you do, too.

Madrone *(Arbutus menziesii)*

If you have explored the Bay Area's forests even to a minor degree, you have probably noticed madrones. These trees stand out because of their bark—a striking dark red that is irresistibly smooth. I love to run my hands over a madrone trunk on a warm day; the polished red surface stays cool. Try resting your cheek against the wood.

In July and August the bark peels off in curls; the tree sheds its old skin. It's fun to pull off the old curls, exposing the new, green bark underneath. Within a few weeks, that fresh layer will have darkened and reddened to the mature bark color.

You can make a pleasant tea with curls of bark. I use about five peels, or what measures about 3 inches by 4 inches when laid out side by side, which seems a good amount for a mugful. Pour boiling water over the bark curls, and by the time the brew is cool enough to drink it will be a lovely cinnamon color. Madrone bark tea tastes a little like Chinese green tea mixed with the fragrance of bark or wood. Its flavor is homey and a little musty, like the smell of a room full of books that has been closed up for a season by the ocean. The tea combines well with many other flavors. It can add bass notes to an herb-tea blend. Or try it straight with milk and honey, or with lemon. Best of all, steep pieces of madrone and cinnamon bark together; the two are natural partners.

Madrone Bark

Madrones bloom in March, April, and early May. The blossoms hang in cascades of small, urn-shaped flowers. They smell like honey and taste mildly sweet. Where large concentrations of madrone trees occur, the air becomes quite fragrant. If you want to experience the full effect of madrones in bloom, a lovely place to go is the madrone grove at the edge of "The Meadows" in Wunderlich County Park, on the Peninsula. One late March, all the trees were in bloom, the meadow was carpeted in fresh grass, and the sweet air was so clear that everything sparkled.

Many madrone trees do not bear fruit, but occasional ones produce scarlet berries that hang in bright clusters all over the tree, set off against the glossy leaves. Although madrone trees bloom as early as March, their berries do not ripen until November or December, an unusually long maturation period. The fully ripe berries are edible and can be quite tasty. They tend to keep a trace of astringency, but some trees produce less puckery berries than others. So if you don't like the first madrone berries you try, don't assume that you won't like others.

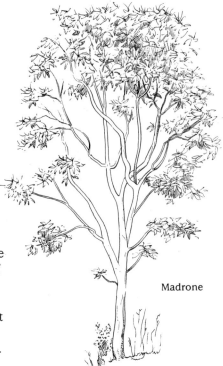

Madrone

Their wonderful color makes them fun to cook with. You might try baking them with meats; one friend suggested using them in a turkey casserole, which sounds promising. I have tried them in two ways, one a failure and the other a definite success. First, the failure. I had heard that one could make a cider with them, similar to manzanita cider (which is delicious). This information was misleading. Pureeing a cup of berries with a cup of water in the blender resulted in a thick mush, so I added another cup of water. The mixture sat in a jar in the refrigerator overnight, and in the morning an inch of cider-colored water floated above the mass of pink berry mash. Manzanita berry cider is fragrant and fruity, but that inch of madrone cider had only the remotest hints of sourness or sweetness. It had virtually no flavor; the only place I could taste it was on the back of my tongue.

I had more luck using madrone berries to make a fruit sauce, which turned out spicy and appetizing (see the recipe). Since these berries are ripe at the peak of the holiday entertaining period, you might enjoy including a native Californian dessert in a festive meal. The pink color and fruity flavor are good enough to hold their own among more traditional foods. Best of all, serving a madrone dessert requires that you first go outdoors and spend some quiet time picking the berries. That's

MADRONE PUDDING OR SAUCE

- madrone berries
- sugar or honey
- cornstarch

- lemon
- ginger

Mash the berries in a saucepan and add just enough water to cover them. Simmer the mixture for about 10 minutes. Then pour the mixture through a sieve, being sure to save all the liquid. Mash the berries gently again, against the mesh of the sieve. Scrape off all the pulp that comes through on the back of the sieve and add it to the liquid. Throw away the berry residue left in the sieve.

Sweeten the sauce with sugar or honey to taste. Add a squeeze of lemon juice and a pinch of ground ginger. To thicken the sauce, use cornstarch. Dissolve each tablespoon of cornstarch in a tablespoon of cold water before stirring it into the sauce. For a cup of sauce, I used 2 tablespoons of cornstarch; you may prefer yours more or less thick. Cook the sauce over low to medium heat for another 10 minutes, stirring occasionally, and then chill it.

The result is an attractive, pale pink, jelled pudding that tastes surprisingly like spiced applesauce, except for the difference in texture. If you fold whipped cream into the pudding, you create a delicious madrone fool.

one of the surest ways to refresh your spirits when the extra pressures of December threaten to cloud your pleasure in the holidays.

Where and When to Find It   Madrones most often grow in wooded areas, particularly in association with Douglas firs, tanoaks, and live oaks. In Marin and on the Peninsula, madrones are common on forested slopes of that type. Nice specimens grow on Bolinas Ridge, on the TCC Trail on Mt. Tamalpais, and on Angel Island. To the south, you can't miss them at the entrance to Castle Rock State Park or at "The Meadows" in Wunderlich County Park.

In the East Bay, they are common in the Berkeley/Hayward hills, but are only occasional as far east as Mt. Diablo. You'll also find them at Niles

Madrone
Berries

Canyon and at Briones, Las Trampas, and Sunol parks. A particularly productive grove grows along Redwood Road between Oakland and Castro Valley. And they are attractive along Interstate 580 through the inner Coast Range.

To sum up, the trees bloom in March through early May, shed their bark in July and August, and develop fully ripe berries by November and December.

Manzanita *(Arctostaphylos* species*)*

Manzanita cider is delicious, and yet the berries that produce it are papery on the outside and dry powder within. When I first picked them, I was incredulous that anything good could come from berries that looked like they were beyond redemption. Fortunately, the glowing reports in foraging books outweighed my food prejudices, and I did not abandon the harvest. Give your taste buds a chance to overrule the evidence of your eyes on this one.

Manzanita is a shrubby plant, native to California, with leathery, evergreen leaves. Its red bark is similar to that of its relative, the madrone: smooth, hard, and sinewy where it is not peeling. The blossoms smell like honey and are urn shaped like those of madrone, huckleberry, and blueberry. All four species are members of the Heath family of plants. The berries look a bit like tiny apples, which is why the Spanish named the plant manzanita, or little apple.

At least eighteen species of manzanita grow in the area covered by this book. Some grow into magnificent shrubs 10 to 20 feet high, whose muscular red wood stands out like a living sculpture. Others are ordinary chest-high bushes, while still others spread along the ground and rise no higher than your knees. While they sound quite different from each other, the family resemblance is actually quite easy to see. Once you can recognize one manzanita, you will be able to recognize the other forms as well. The leaves are always a little stiff, comparatively thick, and have a simple shape. They attach to the branches in a characteristic way, overlapping and sticking out in all directions, giving plants that "manzanita" look no matter what size they are. The berries of all the species can be used for making cider.

Berries are ready to harvest when they are completely dry inside and out. If you pick them earlier, while they are still fleshy, your cider will be disappointing. When the berries are very dry, whole clusters will fall into your hand at the slightest tug, making harvesting relatively simple.

The one tedious part of cooking with manzanita is sorting through the berries to separate out the stems and the diseased or wormy berries. I would suggest doing it as part of your hike. You might as well lean against a tree and have a beautiful view while you sort them. Besides, that way you can avoid the trauma of worms in your kitchen. Once, two tiny grubworms crawled out of the berry pile I was sorting. The sight of worms indoors flooded my system with an unpleasant jolt of adrenalin. Given the choice, I would have hurled beasts and berries alike out the window. If you sort outdoors, even a grub can seem a natural part of the earth's rhythms.

Once the berries are sorted, making the cider is easy. Put the berries in a saucepan with an equal volume of water and boil them for 2 or 3 minutes. Then puree the mixture in a blender, pour it into a jar, and let it sit in the refrigerator for at least a few hours. I shook mine occasionally on the theory that it might increase the flavor extracted from the berry pulp.

When you are ready to drink the cider, pour it through a sieve to remove the berry mash. The cider will be a pale brown with reddish tones, much like the color of unfiltered apple juice but slightly darker. I like mine without sweetener, so taste it before you add any. Manzanita cider is tart and fruity like a good lemonade, with a pleasant flavor all its own.

One useful quality of the berries is that they will stay fresh for months if you store them unwashed in an airtight bag or container in the refrigerator. I picked some in late July and didn't use them until mid-October, when a second harvest gave me enough berries to make a reasonable

Manzanita

quantity of cider. The July crop was still in fine shape; in fact, it looked identical to the freshly gathered batch.

Where and When to Find It   Manzanitas of one species or another grow throughout the Bay Area, from Mt. Diablo to the coastal headlands. You will find them most often in chaparral, but some species inhabit open woods, forest borders, or grassy hillsides. They thrive on dryness; I don't recall ever seeing one near a marsh. Just look for that red bark and you're bound to find them.

Manzanita is one of the earliest-blooming shrubs, adding beauty to winter hikes. I have seen various species in bloom in late November on Bolinas Ridge, in early February on Mt. Tamalpais, and in late March in Butano State Park.

The season for picking the ripe berries is equally long, running from May through October, with August and September as the peak months. The earliest bloomers are not necessarily the earliest bearers; the same shrubs that blossomed on Bolinas Ridge in November were still carrying berries the following October.

Coast or Beach Strawberry *(Fragaria chiloensis)*
California or Woodland Strawberry *(F. californica)*

What is more fitting for a day in late May than to be on your knees among the wildflowers of the coastal headlands eating wild strawberries? Never mind that the fog is probably heavy and that you are bundled in a parka while the rest of the nation is warm. *Fragaria chiloensis,* which is common along our coast, is the species from which strawberries were domesticated, and each fingernail-sized berry is as powerfully sweet and flavorful as strawberry syrup. Surprisingly much flavor was traded for greater size and sturdiness in the creation of a marketable berry.

In moist woods, look for California strawberries. Their berries are not as sweet as the coastal variety, which only means that they taste more like the store-bought kind. Any wild strawberry is delicious.

Infrequently, I have seen mock strawberry plants in the woods. These counterfeit berries are pretty but have no taste at all. Whereas both species of strawberries have white blossoms, the mock strawberry's are yellow. All strawberry plants have leaves in clusters of three.

The berries are extremely easily crushed and neither species bears them in such numbers as to be practical for cooking. But, oh, what sweet memories they will give you of pawing through the leaves in a fruiting patch, uncovering one perfect berry here and then another a foot away. If they are coastal berries, I don't even mind the sand on them, because they are so astonishingly sweet. These low-growing plants are hardy and can withstand your attentions. They reproduce by sending out runners, so you don't have to worry that you are consuming the sources of future happiness. The plants are the principle; the berries are the interest. Life offers few purer pleasures than the leisurely exploration of a producing strawberry patch in the company of a friend.

Coast
Strawberry

California Strawberry

While the normal season for strawberries is late spring, they can ripen much earlier. One January day in the cold and extraordinarily rainy winter of 1982, I was walking at Tennessee Cove. A large slide had swept a chunk of the hillside across the trail. Lots of strawberry plants had made the trip intact, down from the inaccessible slope above. I was amazed to see a fair number of almost ripe berries and thoroughly enjoyed them. They were both tart and sweet at that stage. The slide was later bulldozed away, so I do not know if those plants always produced early or if the trauma of the move had stimulated them into action. But as a result, I always check for berries when I see a patch of strawberry leaves, from January through July.

Tea made from strawberry leaves figures in a number of herbal remedy books for one problem or another. It has a mild, dusky-woods aroma. Be sure to dry the leaves thoroughly before using them. As they wilt, a poison develops in them, but it vanishes by the time they are dry enough to crumble. The tea is said to be best when made with leaves from blooming plants, which are easy enough to find in the spring.

Where and When to Find Them Coast strawberries cover large areas of beach and headland all along the coast. As a partial list, they grow at Point Reyes, near the lighthouse and on the dunes, and at Rodeo Lagoon, Stinson Beach, Tennessee Valley, Ft. Point, Baker Beach, Lands End, Ft. Funston, Shelter Cove, Pedro Point, Pescadero Beach, and Waddell Creek and Beach. They also grow on San Bruno Mountain, so they occur fairly far from the shoreline; but they do not grow in the East

Bay. Some locations produce much more fruit than others. One of the best patches I've seen is within the San Francisco city limits. Just keep your eyes on the ground when walking past the plants and occasionally look under the leaves of a plant or two.

California or woodland strawberries are fairly common and wide-spread throughout the forests of the fog zone. While you'll find plenty of plants in the Berkeley and Oakland hills, they become scarce by the time you go as far east as Mt. Diablo. On the Peninsula and in Marin, they grow in too many places to even attempt a list, but as examples, the plants are common in Butano and Wunderlich parks, Tomales Bay State Park, and wooded portions of Mt. Tamalpais and Point Reyes.

Look for ripe berries in April, May, and June.

Sea Fig *(Carpobrotus chilense,* formerly *Mesembryanthemum chilense)*
Ice Plant *(C. edule,* formerly *M. edule)*

Sea figs and ice plants are a familiar sight to most Bay Area residents. We generally lump them together as ice plants, although that name is actually supposed to belong to another species.

Both sea figs and ice plants have fleshy, triangular leaves that form dense mats of vegetation and often turn deep red in the dry season. The native species, *Carpobrotus chilense,* grows on dunes along the coast. The South African import, *C. edule,* is naturalized along the coast and is widely planted along roads for erosion control.

The plants bloom in spring and early summer. The native flowers are hot pink to purplish rose, while the introduced species can be either yellow or pink. The blossoms of both are large and showy. In late September and early October, the fruits turn red, sometimes perfuming the air with a delicious sweetness. At that point, you can pull the fruits open and eat the seeds and pink goo inside; both are slightly sweet. It's worth doing once, just to get an idea of what's inside the "figs" that are such an odd-looking part of our landscape.

I have read that the triangular leaves of *C. edule* can be used raw in salads. Maybe this is true for some people, but I can't eat them. In fact, one time my mouth burned for half an hour after chewing a leaf. The true ice plant that grows further south is supposed to be tastier. I'd recommend forgetting about the salad idea and just sampling the fig goo.

Sea Fig

Where and When to Find Them   Since freeway road cuts are rotten foraging locations, concentrate your efforts along the East Bay shoreline and along the coast.

If the leaves agree with you, they can be used for salads the year round. The figs ripen in the fall, with peak availability in late September and early October.

Primarily Plums, plus Apples, Figs, and Pears
(*Prunus,* plus *Malus, Ficus,* and *Pyrus* species)

Wild orchards are scattered throughout the Bay Area's public lands, usually near the site of some once-loved home. While we tend not to think of untended fruit trees in the same context as wild edibles, biting into a wild pear, apple, or plum is about as satisfying as foraging gets. The fruit is usually good and sometimes perfect. My favorite orchard afternoon was spent eating ripe figs from a huge, fragrant tree standing by itself in the wheat-colored grass of a dry autumn meadow far from the sound of cars or the sight of other people. A certain crunchy, sweet,

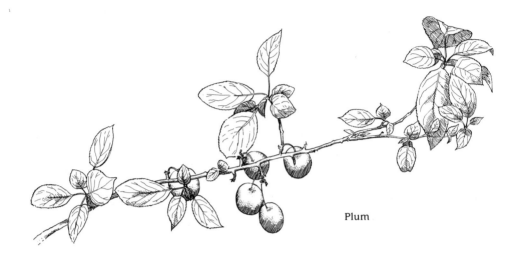

Plum

fat plum from a small, utterly romantic, hidden orchard of plums, pears, apricots, apples, and even a loquat also lingers in memory.

Part of the experience is the wistful sense of connection to the people who once planted the trees and gazed at them contentedly from the windows of a home no longer present. We always tromp around a newly discovered orchard until we determine where we think the house was. Then we stand there and comment on the views. The ritual seems part of paying our respects to people who left, mysteriously—through a "magnificent bequest," a bitter loss to eminent domain, or a satisfied, straightforward sale?—so that the land might be opened to everyone.

Where and When to Find Them   Watch for trees completely swathed in white blossoms in spring; fruit trees are most easily spotted then, exercising their astonishing capacity to cover each twig and branch in flowers. Ripening times will vary with the species and the location; you'll need to check occasionally through the summer and fall.

As ripening approaches, visit the trees as often as you can. My experience with a favorite orchard has been that people will swoop down on it and harvest the trees bare soon after the fruit ripens, so the rest of us have to be on our toes to get a taste of the bounty. Remember that whatever humans don't eat will go to support deer and other animals, so fruit left on the tree isn't wasted.

Given the popularity of these trees, I think I'll stay more vague than usual about locations. Suffice it to say that wild orchards await you in the East Bay Regional Park District, the Golden Gate National Recreation Area, the Midpeninsula Regional Open Space District, and other state, county, and federal spaces. Just keep hiking new trails in the spring and you will discover them.

Bugle or Western Golden Currant *(Ribes gracillimum)*
Chaparral or California Black Currant *(R. malvaceum)*
Flowering or Pink-flowering Currant *(R. sanguineum,* also *R. glutinosum)*
California or Hillside Gooseberry *(R. californicum)*
Canyon Gooseberry *(R. menziesii)*
Spreading or Straggly Gooseberry *(R. divaricatum)*

Currants and gooseberries are easily identified as a group by their three-lobed leaves (or in a few species, three dominant lobes and two much smaller ones). Also, blossom remnants remain attached like tails to the berries. Currant branches and berries are smooth. Gooseberry branches always have spines, and in most species the berries are covered with short spines as well.

The Bay Area has a wealth of both types of fruit. Of the currants, the western golden currant tastes best. Its berries are red and orange when ripe. If they are too sour to be eaten out-of-hand, you can make a fruit sauce or other sweetened dessert with them.

The pink-flowering currant is renowned for its blossoms. My favorite bush along the coast begins flowering in February, but a friend has seen the blossoms elsewhere as early as December. They hang in showy pink and white clusters from the branches. Both this currant and the chaparral currant produce blue-black berries that taste slightly bitter and resinous, with a trace of sweetness. Drying them in a very low oven (150° to 200° F.) until they are shriveled and dry to the touch slightly increases their sweetness. Dried currants will keep almost indefinitely.

The gooseberries are more of a bother to harvest because of the spines, but their berries also taste better. One, the straggly gooseberry, does have smooth-skinned berries, but its branches have the usual spines. California gooseberry is my favorite of the entire *Ribes* clan. It produces very sweet-fleshed, purple-skinned berries. You can enjoy them on the trail by peeling the skin away from the pulp (pull on the spines) and eating the insides as is.

When you harvest gooseberries (as with most wild fruits), it is very important to choose fully ripe ones. Perfectly ripe, the local gooseberries are sweet and very good, but even a few unripe ones will contribute their bitterness to any gooseberry dishes you create. They should be deep purple or black.

A gooseberry's attachment to the stem will dry and weaken by the time the berry is fully ripe. Sometimes, it has weakened enough that you can pick the berry just by pulling on its tail. If it won't come off, then you must gingerly tug on the berry itself, trying to get as few spines in your fingers as possible. Gloves help.

The simplest, best way I've found to enjoy the berries and cope with their spines is to make a gooseberry fool. Put the fully ripe berries in a saucepan and barely cover them with water. Crush them. (A potato masher or the bottom of a glass jar works well.) Simmer gently for about 5 minutes. Put the mixture through a sieve, pressing the berries well to extract as much pulp as possible. Throw away the berry skins and then scrape the pulp off the back of the sieve and add it to the berry sauce. Add sugar to taste. Add cornstarch (start with a tablespoon and use more if necessary, dissolving it first in a little cold water), and gently simmer the sauce, stirring, until it thickens. Chill the sauce. It should develop a pudding consistency.

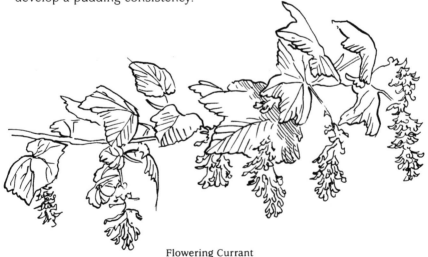

Flowering Currant

Made with purple gooseberries, the sauce is a striking magenta red and has a pleasant sweet and tart taste somewhat like rhubarb. The flavor is so concentrated that I fold the sauce into whipped cream to extend and mute it. The resulting gooseberry fool is charmingly pink and delicious.

Where and When to Find Them

Bugle or Western Golden Currant   Look along streams in canyons from Alameda County south in the East Bay. It also grows in southern San Mateo County, as well as the northern portions of Santa Clara and Santa Cruz counties. It is unfortunately not common in any of these areas, and does not occur at all in Marin. It blooms in February and March and fruits in summer.

Chaparral or California Black Currant   Its favored habitat is the edge of chaparral or bushy slopes, primarily on dry hillsides. In Marin it is rare but does grow on the south face of Mt. Tamalpais. It also grows in scattered locations on the Peninsula. The interior parts of the East Bay, such as Briones, Las Trampas, and Mt. Diablo parks, are probably the best places to find this currant. Its showy, mildly fragrant flowers bloom from October through March, enriching winter walks. The berries ripen in May and June.

Flowering or Pink-flowering Currant   This one is a fog zone plant. It grows in the Berkeley Hills, and is common near streams, in moist woods, or on moist, bushy slopes in San Francisco and on the Peninsula. In Marin, Howell (*Marin Flora*) reports it from Rodeo Lagoon, Sausalito, Mt. Tam, Ross Valley, Stinson Beach, Inverness, and Ledum Swamp on the Point Reyes Peninsula. It generally flowers from late January through April, and bears fruit in early summer.

California or Hillside Gooseberry   This shrub grows in wooded areas, in open chaparral, or on grassy hillsides. In Marin, it appears occasionally; Howell notes it at Lake Lagunitas, in San Anselmo Canyon, in Lucas Valley, and at Tomales Bay State Park. It also grows on Angel Island. It is widespread throughout the East Bay; when you find gooseberries in Briones, Las Trampas, and other nearby parks, they are probably this species. On the Peninsula, it grows on San Bruno Mountain in Pilarcitos Canyon, and on Coal Mine Ridge, among other places.

California gooseberry blooms from January through April. By March

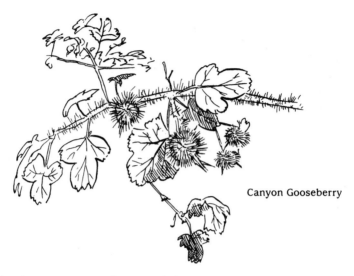

Canyon Gooseberry

many bushes are setting fruit. Look for ripe berries in May and June; in Briones, for example, the peak time is early to mid-June.

Canyon Gooseberry   This species favors moist woods, especially on north-facing slopes. Occasional in Marin, it does grow on Mt. Tam and at Point Reyes, on the Sky and Bear Valley trails. On the Peninsula, it grows from San Francisco southward, and appears at Big Basin and along Waddell Creek. This is the most common gooseberry in the Berkeley/Hayward hills, and though there is less of it to the east, it is relatively common on the highest northern slopes of Mt. Diablo. This species, *Ribes menziesii,* is undergoing a taxonomic identity crisis, and is sometimes divided up and given other names. If you can't find it in a flora, look for *R. menziesii* listed as a synonym in the fine print. It blooms from March through June (sometimes August!), depending, as always, on the location. Thus, fruiting time is also very long. I found some ripe, sweet gooseberries at Pescadero Creek County Park in late September once, and they were most likely this species.

Spreading or Straggly Gooseberry   Look for this one near streams or marshy areas, often in shade and among other water-loving shrubs, like willows. Somewhat rare in Marin, it grows in the Fern Creek and Cataract Creek areas of Mt. Tam and at Mad Lake and Drake's Estero at Point Reyes. It is occasional from San Francisco southward. I can find no reports of it growing in the East Bay. It blooms from February through May, so look for fruit from May to July.

Wild or Wood Rose *(Rosa gymnocarpa)*
California Rose *(R. californica)*
Sweetbriar or Eglantine *(R. rubiginosa)*
Sonoma Rose *(R. spithamea)*

Rose hips, the red fruits that follow the blossoms, achieved fame during World War II when the English gathered them from garden and countryside as a rich source of Vitamin C for their inadequate wartime diet. The hips were (and still are) made into tablets by pharmaceutical companies and distributed to the public. Rose hips can also be eaten directly with less vitamin loss and a reasonable degree of pleasure.

Recipes for rose hips abound. *Joy of Cooking* includes one for jam and mentions their use in tea. Wild-food books recommend using them for soups, fruit leathers, purees, syrups, and in baked goods.

Why are they so popular? In part because they are easy to harvest. A rose bush can bear hundreds of hips, mostly on the tips of the stems; they can be snapped off without too much contact between human and thorn. In part because their color is beautiful and they are so relaxingly familiar. And their flavor is bland enough to take on whatever character one wants to give it, with the addition of sugar and spices.

I confess to being no great fan of rose-hip foods, since they usually need a fair amount of sugar to taste good. They give me more pleasure

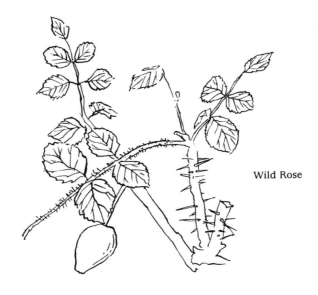

Wild Rose

on the bush, shining scarlet in a season when all around them is tan and brown and color is scarce. When I can find firm, flavorful hips, I do like to nibble a few in the field. It's fun to try to eat the fleshy part without breaking the membrane that surrounds the inner seeds. And some fresh hips do have the mildly tart, apple flavor ascribed to them.

However, Bay Area rose hips have a tendency to be mushy and taste-less, especially after they have been ripe for a while. Taste a hip before you collect from a bush; if it is mushy, there won't be much flavor in any foods you prepare from that harvest. Sometimes neighboring bushes vary substantially in the quality of their fruit.

For any rose-hip recipe, you need to remove the stems and the dried material on the blossom end. To make a soup, puree, syrup, or leather, put the hips in a saucepan with water to barely cover and simmer them for 10 minutes. Then pour the mixture through a strainer, collecting the liquid and mashing the hips to collect all the pulp. Alternately, you can puree the hips, seeds and all, in a blender with a little water until the mixture is smooth.

For a puree to use as a spread: Sweeten the puree to taste. Spray a cookie sheet with Pam or a similar coating material. Pour the puree on the sheet and keep in a very low oven (150° to 200° F.) until the leather is dry. This can take up to 24 hours. Keep the oven door propped open an inch. When the puree has become leathery, roll it up, wrap it tightly, and freeze it until you are ready to eat it.

For syrup, to use on pancakes, etc.: Add water to the puree to desired consistency. Heat with one part honey or sugar to two parts rose-hip mixture, until the sweetener is dissolved and evenly distributed. Then refrigerate.

For soup: Add extra water to the puree so that the total volume of water is twice the original volume of the rose hips. For example, if you began with 2 cups rose hips, use 1 quart of water to make the soup, counting the water used to make the puree. Add sugar to taste. Add 1 tablespoon cornstarch per quart of soup, dissolving the cornstarch first in cool water. Heat the soup gently, stirring until it becomes clear again and begins to thicken. It can be served hot or cold, and is improved by a splash of cherry or orange liqueur. The rose hips contribute more color than flavor.

To make rose-hip tea: Assuming you will use a perforated tea egg or some other strainer to make the tea, you can skip the tedious process of removing the seeds. Just split the rose hips in half and dry them in pie tins or on a cookie sheet, as described for the fruit leather. The drying will take only 15 to 30 minutes in this case. When the hips are fully dry, seal them in an airtight bag or container; they will keep almost indefinitely.

To make a cup of tea, first pour hot water in a cup to warm it, then discard that water. Put at least 1 tablespoon of dried hips in the cup, and pour boiling water over them. Let them steep for 3 to 5 minutes before removing them. Add sugar to taste. This tea is a warm orange color and tastes mildly fruity.

Note: A few people are powerfully allergic to rose hips, and you won't know whether you are until you've tried them. So don't eat many the first time.

The wood rose is a delicate shrub, with small leaves, blossoms, and fruits. The bushes grow singly, and usually have at most three or four hips on them, which glow like tiny jewels in the forest shade. To harvest enough rose hips for cooking, you will want to find a sturdy specimen of the California rose or the eglantine rose, a European immigrant. Both grow into large, full bushes that bear flowers and fruit in abundance. The eglantine rose is so aggressive and tenacious that it is considered a noxious weed by some, although its flowers are lovely.

Rose hips are fun enough to cook with, but I would rather spend the time smelling the flowers that preceded them. The most fragrant species of wild rose, like the Eglantine, have a warmth and power to their sweetness that cultivated varieties do not approach.

Wild Rose

Where and When to Find Them   You will see the wood rose in woods throughout the Bay Area. The Sonoma rose is also petite and grows in Marin and on the Peninsula in high chaparral and open woodlands.

The eglantine grows in low, coastal pastures in Marin. The California rose grows throughout the Bay Area, especially on sunny stream banks, but also on dunes, headlands, and in woods. I've seen this species covered in ripe hips on Angel Island and in Briones Park. But the very best place to go for a rose-hip harvest is Grizzly Island in Suisun Marsh. The roses thrive in that habitat, lining sections of road and levee in an unbroken hedge.

All the local rose species bloom from about April to September. August and September are the best months to gather the hips. In this climate, winter's cool weather does not make them sweeter; it only leaves them waterlogged.

Thimbleberry *(Rubus parviflorus)*

Ah, thimbleberries. Choicest of the Bay Area's wild fruits, they look and taste like raspberries, but are sweeter and grow on a thornless bush. Mention thimbleberries to people who have eaten them and their features will soften with happy memories.

Thimbleberry

In the Bay Area, it is rare to find more than a few ripe berries per bush. Further north along the coast, the bushes are supposed to be much more prolific. The shrubs at this latitude seem to put their energy into large, slightly fuzzy, maple-shaped leaves, against which their large, white blossoms stand out. The berries that follow may look tempting when they are pink, but they are unripe. Wait until they darken to a vibrant coral. Even if only one or two have achieved that state of grace when I pass by, their flavor is so superb that I feel I've been handed a treasure.

Where and When to Find It   Thimbleberry shrubs are common along streams, in coastal scrub, and in redwood forests. They form large thickets on moist, shady slopes in the fog zone, as, for example, along Sir Francis Drake Boulevard as it enters Inverness in Marin. I have also seen many bushes at Pescadero Creek County Park on the Peninsula and Tomales Bay State Park in Marin.

In the East Bay, the shrubs are rare on Mt. Diablo, occasional along streams in Briones and similar parks, and common in the Berkeley/Hayward hills.

Most flowers bloom in May, though they begin in March and linger through August. Peak thimbleberry season is normally mid-June to mid-July throughout the Bay Area.

Himalaya Berry *(Rubus discolor,* formerly *R. procerus)*
California or Trailing Blackberry *(R. ursinus)*

Blackberries are wildly abundant here, spilling over fences and covering hillsides. But immigrants from other parts of the United States find that their initial delight in such bounty often dims. Blackberries need both heat and rain in summer to reach their best. Neither the dry warmth inland nor the cool coastal fogs meet those requirements.

However, it is always worth tasting at least one ripe blackberry in every patch you pass. Remember that any red segments make for very sour berries; they must be black all over to be at their best. Often, even ripe berries will be sour or seedy, but some thickets do get enough of the right conditions to produce fine berries. The best blackberries frequently grow beside streams, where their roots can find the moisture that our summer climate does not provide.

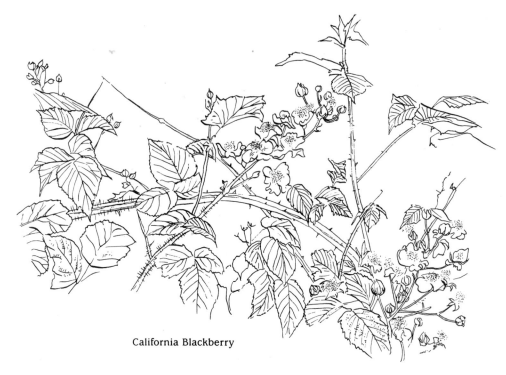

California Blackberry

And what joy there is in finding a good crop! A proper blackberry is juicy, sweet, fruity, and tart in near-perfect proportions. And where one grows, usually you'll find enough others to make a cobbler or pie, or simply to feast on to your heart's content. There's nothing stingy about a blackberry thicket.

Indeed, Himalaya berries, which are the sweeter of the two local species, are considered an aggressive weed. Originally from Europe, the vine invades wild land as well as waste places and roadsides. As a result, the usual caveats about where one should and should not eat wild foods do not apply to blackberries. As one ranger in the Golden Gate National Recreation Area said, "*Please* pick the blackberries. The vines just spread and spread." Even in Tilden Park, where most foraging near the Nature Center is strongly discouraged, the blackberry patch by the Little Farm is fair game.

Blackberry leaves can be used to make tea. Straight, their flavor is not notable, but in an herbal blend, they contribute an attractive green color. As with strawberry leaves, they contain toxins when wilted that disappear when they are fully dried. Be sure to dry the leaves to the crumbly stage before using them.

Even the sourest-berried thickets contribute to the loveliness of our springtimes. A blackberry bramble in bloom is exuberantly beautiful. The white and pale pink flowers cluster in curving sprays of great delicacy. They are at their best in May and sometimes into June.

Where and When to Find Them   Himalaya berries have larger, more rounded leaflets than the native shrub, and their leaflets generally grow in clusters of five. They are common and widespread in Marin and San Francisco. They also grow along urban streams and near the Bay in the East Bay, and in thickets on Grizzly Island.

California blackberries generally produce three leaflets to a stem. They are common in San Francisco, on the Peninsula, and in Marin. In the East Bay, they are widespread in woodlands but are not very productive.

For a few fine locations to get your berrying career off to a good start, try Point Pinole in the East Bay, Mt. Davidson in San Francisco, and Muir Beach in Marin.

Most of the berries ripen in July, August, and September.

California Blackberry

Blue Elderberry *(Sambucus coerula)*

Blue elderberries grow as shrubby trees with finely toothed leaflets arranged in groups of five to nine per stem. In spring they are covered with large, white flower clusters, followed by equally large clusters of edible, blue berries.

Elderberries are an excellent forager's plant, but they also have been used extensively for music making. The pith is soft, so the wood is easily hollowed. California Indians and Mediterranean shepherds and many others carved their flutes from it.

The plant has also been used for numerous folk remedies. The one that impressed me most came from a level-headed expert on the Indian uses of plants. He is quite sensitive to bee stings. He was stung once near an elderberry and so experimented by rubbing the sting with the tree's leaves. He says the sting, which had instantly begun to swell, flattened back down and he didn't experience any of the usual allergic reactions.

In spring, the tree's large, creamy flowers are wonderfully fragrant, with a heavy, uncomplicated sweetness similar to a privet's. The flowers are edible, tasting like a cross between a flower and a vegetable, an unusual but decent flavor. When the blossoms are fully open, try bending the flowering umbel into a plastic bag and shaking it gently or stroking it lightly. If you do this correctly, you can collect the tiny but abundant petals without disturbing the centers of each flower, where the berries will form.

Mixed into pancakes or muffins, the petals add moisture, lightness, and a slight fragrance. They also give an intriguing flavor to fritters. Some people dip entire flower clusters into batter and deep-fry them as a sort of flower-filled doughnut. Dried, the petals can be brewed into tea. Adding a mint leaf or two makes a pleasant variation in the flavor.

Note: It is important to distinguish between blue elderberries and red elderberries, since *the red species is poisonous.* (I have read of people being poisoned by playing their elderberry flutes; presumably they were carved from red elderberry wood.) When you are collecting the berries, it's easy: take only blue ones. Red elderberries turn red when ripe, as you might have guessed. When the plants are in bloom, you can tell which is which by the shape of the flowering clusters. The flowers of the blue elderberry grow in a flattened, saucerlike cluster, resembling a Japanese parasol opened wide. Red elderberry blossoms grow in a

Blue Elderberry

mound, with a clear dome shape that looks more like an upside-down cup than a saucer. Also, red elderberries almost always grow along streams that flow directly into the ocean. It is definitely a coastal species, whereas blue elderberry grows all over the Bay Area. Novices may want to gather blossoms only from trees in dry inland areas.

Blue elderberries are juicy and abundant, but vary dramatically in flavor from shrub to shrub. Some taste fine, while others, equally ripe, are inedible, with a bitterness that no recipe can expunge. The cardinal rule in gathering them is to taste first. If you like the flavor of the raw berry,

Red Elderberry
(poisonous)

ELDERBERRY SYRUP

- blue elderberries
- sugar or honey
- lemon
- cornstarch

First measure, then crush, the elderberries in a saucepan. Add water in the proportion of ¾ cup water to every cup of elderberries. Simmer the mixture for 15 minutes and then strain it, pouring the liquid through twice to extract as much flavor as possible from the berries in the sieve. Discard the berries. Add sugar or honey to taste, along with some fresh lemon juice—try ¼ lemon for every cup of berries. Add cornstarch, 1 teaspoon per cup of berries; dissolve it first in a little cold water. Simmer the syrup, stirring it gently, until it begins to thicken. Then pour it into a container and refrigerate it.

The syrup is a magnificent purplish red color. Even if you haven't eaten pancakes in a decade, it is worth making a batch as an excuse to enjoy the syrup. It is also good on yogurt or ice cream.

then cooking will make it even better. But if its flavor bothers you, gathering more from that plant is probably a waste of time and berries.

Drying the berries before cooking them is supposed to remove the trace of rankness that even good ones can harbor. However, it will not remove bitterness, if it is present.

So much for the bad berries. There are plenty in the Bay Area that taste sweet and fruity; and if you look, you will find them with relative ease. The trees are widespread and common.

When the berries are ripe, they become a deep blue covered with a whitish bloom. The overall appearance is light blue and very pretty. After you find a blue elderberry with tasty berries, the harvest is easier than for any other local berry. The entire cluster, heavy with fruit, snaps off readily without harm to the plant.

At home, the simplest way to sort the berries is to pick them over while they are still attached to the umbels. Probably many will have come loose in the bag. Just put them in a pot of water, stir once or twice, and the shriveled berries and twigs will float to the surface where you can skim them off. Repeat the process a few times.

What to do with them? *Joy of Cooking* gives a recipe for elderberry jam. Elderberry wine is also a traditional American creation. I like elderberries best made into syrup or pies. Whatever you make will be good for you because the berries are rich in Vitamin C.

If you dry the berries in a low oven to remove the mildly rank flavor, rehydrate them by simmering them briefly with a little water, sugar, and lemon. The result is stewed elderberries, tasty as is but also delicious as pie filling. Pies made this way are said to taste even better than those made with fresh berries.

Where and When to Find It   Blue elderberry is a shrub or small tree that thrives on warmth, so it is usually more common away from the immediate coast. Its favored habitats include open woods, brushy or grass-covered hillsides, and streambanks.

Basically, it is not demanding or fussy in its requirements and is widespread from the fog zone to the Delta. Three places where I have found good fruit are on Angel Island, in Briones Park, and on Mt. Diablo, but dreadful berries grow in these parks as well. If you don't like what you taste, move on to the next shrub! Countless prime harvests await your discovery.

The blossoms are at their best from mid-April through June, and their perfume can be one of the most memorable parts of a spring wildflower walk. Look for the berries in July and August. It may be a coincidence, but the ones I've found in September and October have always been bitter.

Evergreen Huckleberry *(Vaccinium ovatum)*

Evergreen
Huckleberry

Just thinking of huckleberries is relaxing. They are a dependable, democratic berry. Their flavor pleases most people, and enough berries grow here to supply every piemaker who's willing to harvest them.

Huckleberry shrubs grow 3 to 7 feet tall and have small, stiff, shiny leaves that stay dark green the year round. The blossoms are pale pink or white and bell shaped, and the berries turn blue-black when ripe. Basically, they look like blueberries, only smaller, shinier, and darker. Sometimes they are covered with a white bloom that makes them look light blue.

What tranquil afternoons I have spent at Point Reyes, absorbed in the pleasant tedium of trying to fill a bag with those tiny, dark berries. Except when we compare sacks to see who's ahead, my husband and I are each on our own in the shrubbery, listening to bird calls and letting our thoughts run free. I love to look up and see the ocean sparkling in the distance; thoughts of its long horizons and expansive beaches balance the forest's myriad close-up details. The sunlight makes the grasses shine in the hidden meadow where we eat our lunch. Every breeze finds a voice as it passes through the fir branches high overhead.

Sooner or later, one of us gets bored and is ready to move on. With luck it hits us at the same time, so that neither has to feel like the martyred nature lover. An hour or two of picking is all we need to recapture what we came for. Which is what? Basically, it is time spent outdoors without an agenda—who cares how many berries we pick? Without deep conversation, or small talk, or any real interaction with another human bundle of desires and demands. Without a certain mileage to be covered, or a need to match paces, or a plant or animal to be found and observed. And because picking the berries is an accomplishment, no matter how small, it frees me from the feeling that I need to make the time count by thinking about something important or making plans. When I pick huckleberries, I just exist, like a kid floating through summer vacation.

Maybe you find berry picking fun, or even tedious, but not a transcendent experience. No matter. At least you come home with a bag of

---

TRIPLE FRUIT PIE

- pie crust
- 1 pippin or other tart apple
- 1½ cups of Concord grapes
- cornstarch
- 1½ lemons
- a cup or so of huckleberries
- ⅓ to ½ cup sugar

Preheat the oven to 450° F. Line a pie pan with any type of crust. Cut the apple into thin slices and cover the bottom of the pie crust with them. Slip the skins off the grapes and reserve the skins. Cook the grape pulp for a minute or two to soften it, and put it through a sieve to remove the seeds. Dissolve 3 tablespoons cornstarch in the juice of ½ lemon, plus a little water, if necessary. Mix together the huckleberries, the grape pulp and skins, the cornstarch and lemon, and the sugar—I like tart foods and use only ⅓ cup; using ⅔ cup produces a normal, sweet pie. Pour the mixture over the apple slices.

Bake the pie at 450° F. for 10 minutes, and then bake it at 350° for another 40 to 45 minutes. The grapes contribute sweetness and rich flavor, the apple adds body and texture, and the little huckleberries give a contrasting texture and their own tartness. Other wonderful combinations are huckleberries with peaches or mangos.

---

berries—extremely valuable berries, considering the time you have invested in harvesting them—and now you want to make something delicious with them.

First, you need to pull off any green stems that are still attached. Then put the berries in a pot of water. Swish them around and bits of stem or leaf will float to the top along with the tiny, green berries. Strain those off and then pick out any red, unripe berries. Cleaning and sorting them can be a tiresome chore; do it in good company, if possible.

Any blueberry recipe can be used for huckleberries, except that you will need to add more sugar to get the same effect because huckleberries are more tart. You may find the taste of pure huckleberry desserts slightly thin: sweet and sour but without any depth. My appreciation for the berries increased dramatically when I began cooking them with other fruits. The recipes for fruit pie and dessert sauce are two that we have enjoyed.

I used to work for a lawyer named Barbara Phillips. One night, she invited my husband and me over for dinner, and we brought huckleberries as our contribution to the meal. For dessert, I began making a simple, straightforward sauce with them, to go over her homemade yogurt. Barbara tasted it, her mind started ticking, and soon she had transformed it into something far more subtle and exciting. I have regarded huckleberries—and fruit sauces—with a new appreciation after that night.

Where and When to Find It   Marin and the Peninsula are the places to go for huckleberries; they are a coastal species. Huckleberry Preserve is the only place in the East Bay where the bushes thrive. It is a good place to learn what they look like and to taste a few, but if you're after a pie's worth, leave those unique shrubs alone and head for the coast.

The best-bearing plants are usually on ridges or hillsides. For example, at Portola State Park I noticed disappointingly few berries on the shrubs down along a stream, but only a quarter of a mile up the trail, on the ridge, the berries were numerous.

In Marin, the most famous huckleberrying sites are the slopes of Mt. Wittenburg at Point Reyes, Tomales Bay State Park, and Bolinas Ridge. The TCC Trail on the slopes of Mt. Tamalpais is productive, and they also grow in the San Rafael Hills, Lagunitas Canyon, Taylor State Park, and on San Geronimo Ridge.

On the Peninsula, you really can't go wrong in any of the redwood

HUCKLEBERRY DESSERT SAUCE EXTRAORDINAIRE

- 1 cup huckleberries
- sugar or honey
- cornstarch
- 1 lemon
- Cointreau

Put aside ⅓ of the huckleberries. Put the other ⅔ in a saucepan, crush them with the bottom of a jar or other blunt object, and add barely enough water to cover them. Cook, stirring, over low heat, adding sugar or honey to taste. Add cornstarch, dissolved in a little water, 1 tablespoon at a time, until the sauce reaches the thickness you desire. After each tablespoon, stir for a few minutes to see what effect it has on the thickness, before adding more.

When the texture is right, add the uncrushed berries. Remove the peel and white rind from a lemon and cut the pulp into small pieces, adding them to the sauce. You'd think that extra tartness would be the last thing huckleberries needed, but the lemon is a tremendous addition.

Finally, stir in some spoonfuls of Cointreau to taste. This orange-flavored liqueur adds warmth, depth, and interest to the sauce, transforming it remarkably. The wild and civilized flavors bring out the best in each other. Bon appetit!

parks; I have seen lots of bushes at Portola, Pescadero Creek, Butano, and Big Basin parks. The upper slopes of San Bruno Mountain also produce some berries.

Because they are so abundant, huckleberries are unusually dependable. No matter what the weather, you can count on finding some. But the quantity and quality of berries vary a lot from year to year. After the extraordinarily wet winter of 1981–1982, for example, they were more grainy and sour than usual, and the small crop was mostly gone by August. In other years, equally unusual, you'll find enough berries in late November to make pies for Thanksgiving.

In a typical year, the shrubs bloom from February through June. The first ripe berries appear in mid-July, but the great huckleberry months are August, September, and October. The heavy coastal fogs of June and July have broken up by then, and you can usually count on sunny weather for your huckleberrying expedition. If you live in the fog zone, there's nothing like a September afternoon spent berry picking to make summer seem real again, and not just a sweet memory from other places and other times.

California or Wild Grape *(Vitis californica)*

Wild grapes and idyllic settings seem to go together. The vines I have found climb up into the trees near streams, in quiet valleys surrounded by hills. The grapes ripen in September and October when almost every day has perfect weather for strolling along a trail. Eating grapes to my heart's content, listening to the creek flow, and basking in warm, late afternoon sunshine, my cup does feel like it runneth over. I have learned to love this area's autumn smell of dust, coyote brush, and dry grasses. I stand by the vines, smelling, hearing, seeing, and tasting wonderful things, and quiver inside; an animal almost overwhelmed by such intense contentment.

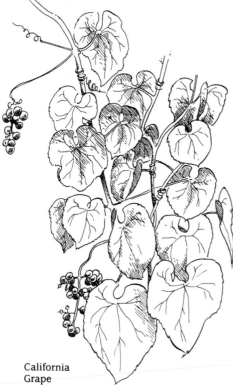

California Grape

You'll find three varieties of fruit on the vines: large, small, and raisins. Surprisingly, the smaller ones are sweeter and less seedy than the big ones. The grapes that have dried on the vine are sweetest of all.

Have you ever eaten a whole pineapple, including the core, and burned your mouth with the acid? Wild grapes create the same effect. When the corners of my mouth start to go numb and tingle, I know it's time to stop.

Some people gather wild grapes for cooking, but when I tried it, I didn't like seeing the jewellike clusters in my kitchen, so far from their sunny valley. There's something about grapes that is particularly primeval; it's easy to imagine Adam and Eve stuffing themselves with the fruit. Wild grapes just seem to belong outside.

Where and When to Find It   Not surprisingly, wild grapes grow best in Napa and Sonoma counties, where they blanket whole trees, especially along streams. In Marin, Howell (*Marin Flora*) found them only in Ignacio, near a railroad track. I haven't seen or heard of them anywhere on the Peninsula. In the East Bay, some vines do well at Briones Park, and they grow in a dozen places on Mt. Diablo, including Mitchell Canyon.

The tiny, green flowers bloom in May and June. In mid-September, you can find ripe grapes and raisins mixed in with the green fruit. By mid-October, the grapes are fully ripe and their leaves have begun to turn crimson around the edges. In early November, the leaf centers turn gold, so the vines become banks of dark, rich color. When they are backlit by the low afternoon sun, they burn with beauty.

BERRIES THAT DO OR MIGHT TASTE GOOD BUT ARE HARD TO FIND

The berries that follow are uncommon harvests in this area. The plants themselves may be common enough, but most don't bear. I've seen many mahonia bushes, for example, but discovered only one location where they produced fruit.

Some of these species I've found and some I'm still looking for. Searching for them will be frustrating to most people who try. But a species that is uncommon or barren throughout most of the Bay Area might fruit heavily in one particular place near you. If so, that species is as abundant for your purposes as blackberries, and this book would serve you poorly if it did not alert you to the plant's potential delights.

Service Berry or Juneberry *(Amelanchier pallida)*

This is supposed to be a delicious berry; I still haven't found any, so I don't know. The bushes tend to be about 3 feet high, though they can grow much larger. The leaves are smooth edged up to the middle and

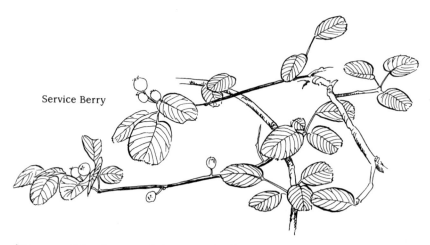

Service Berry

have small teeth around the outer half. Service berries are most conspicuous from April through June, when they bear clusters of white flowers. The berries look a bit like blueberries and are good fresh or dried.

Where and When to Find It   To read all the places listed in the floras, you'd think that service berry would be easy to find, but only a few bushes grow in each place. It is not common anywhere in the Bay Area.

The floras are unusually varied in their descriptions of the typical habitats for the plant. Several mention rocky outcrops on open hillsides and the edges of woods as the likeliest locations. However, the plants also seem to need moisture. *Flora of the Santa Cruz Mountains* describes them as "occasional along streams and on moist slopes, less frequent on the western, ocean-side slopes of the Santa Cruz Mountains than on the eastern. . . ." *Native Shrubs of the San Francisco Bay Region* upholds the moisture idea but contradicts the west/east description, saying they are "often seen on coastal cliffs in the northern counties or around freshwater ponds behind the dunes."

They are uncommon in the East Bay. They do grow in Las Trampas, Briones, Tilden, and Chabot parks, but fruit lightly. In San Francisco they are rare. On the Peninsula they are occasional, which means they are there in reasonable numbers but you'll still need luck to find them. Keep your eyes peeled when you are on San Bruno Mountain, Black Mountain, or Page Mill Road. *Marin Flora* lists the following locations: "Sausalito; Tiburon; Mount Tamalpais (Rock Spring, Rifle Camp,

Lake Lagunitas); San Anselmo Canyon; San Geronimo; San Rafael Hills; Salmon Creek School; Drake's Estero, Point Reyes Peninsula; Tomales."

If your eyes prove sharper and your choice of trails luckier than mine, you should find ripe berries in mid- to late summer. If you see any berries in the autumn that have dried on the bush, those are considered a delicacy as well. And if it wouldn't be too much trouble, would you please send a postcard telling me where to look?

Oregon Grape or Long-leaf Mahonia
(Berberis nervosa)
Shiny-leaf Mahonia *(B. pinnata)*

The mahonias are tantalizing. Finding the shrubs is fairly easy and the berries make a superior fruit syrup or jelly. However, finding a shrub with berries on it is a major challenge.

Mahonia leaves remind me of holly; they are evergreen, stiff, and have very sharp points along their edges. On the coastal headlands or other rocky, exposed areas, *Berberis pinnata* grows as a low shrub, rarely more than a foot or two high. *Berberis nervosa* grows taller, especially in the redwood groves that are its prime habitat. The berries appear in conspicuous clusters. They are deep blue, covered with a whitish bloom. Raw, they taste extremely sour, but a little sugar improves them dramatically.

If you find some mahonia berries, here's how to make a superb syrup: Cook the berries in a saucepan with just enough water to barely cover them. Simmer gently for about 5 minutes. As the softened berries continue to cook, crush them with a spoon to release their juice. Simmer for about 15 minutes in all. Then pour the mixture through a strainer, pressing the berries to extract as much juice as possible.

Sweeten the strained liquid to taste. If you want it thicker, mix in

Oregon Grape

a little cornstarch and cook the mixture gently until it thickens. I like it without extra thickening. The syrup is a deep cerise or magenta color, both tart and sweet, and is wonderful over yogurt, vanilla ice cream, or pancakes.

Where and When to Find Them   *Berberis nervosa* appears only occasionally, and only in Marin or on the Peninsula on steep canyonsides in coniferous forests. The only place I have seen bushes with fruit was among redwoods. In Marin it grows in Muir Woods, on Mt. Tamalpais, and in the Marin Municipal Water District lands. On the Peninsula, look for it in all the redwood parks; it definitely grows along Butano and Waddell creeks.

Berberis pinnata is far more common, but I have yet to see a berry on one plant in this area. It does fruit heavily elsewhere in its range. Who knows? You might be luckier. You'll find the bushes on rocky outcrops. In the East Bay, look at the high elevations of Garin Park, the Berkeley Hills, and Rocky Ridge in Las Trampas Park.

In Marin and on the Peninsula, you will see it most frequently on exposed ridgetops close to the ocean. For example, lots of very low bushes grow on the ridge between Tennessee Valley and Ft. Cronkite and on the ocean side of the upper slopes of San Bruno Mountain.

Mahonias produce clusters of bright yellow flowers from March through May. The berries ripen in mid-summer; if you notice a blooming bush in the spring, check it for fruit during the second half of July.

Salal *(Gaultheria shallon)*

Salal berries are bland but pleasant. In that regard, they are more like commercial berries than any of the other wild species, which tend to have strong, distinctive flavors.

The foliage distinguishes the plant. The handsome leathery leaves are much in demand by florists; in fact, there was a time when sprays of salal were being stolen from parklands in commercial quantities. Fortunately, those days seem to be over.

Finding the berries is not easy. Most of the salal shrubs I have seen give no indication of ever blooming or bearing fruit. From time to time, I find a bush with berries on it and enjoy them raw. However, salal occasionally grows in productive thickets, and if you find such a spot, you can make a good pie with the fruit.

The dark blue berries dangle in loose clusters from the ends of the stems. When the berries on a sprig are ripe, the tip of the sprig, with all the fruit on it, will break off neatly with a gentle tug (or sometimes just a touch). Collecting these sprigs is the best way to harvest salal. Since the berries themselves are very soft and easily crushed, it is better not to handle them until you are ready to cook with them.

Back at home, pinch the berries off at the base of their stems rather than pulling on them. Pulling usually mashes or skins them. Any blueberry recipe works well for salal; just as with blueberries, cooking them with some lemon juice or a tart fruit improves the flavor.

Where and When to Find It   The only area where I have seen salal berries in collectible quantities was in northern Marin County. They occur from Santa Barbara to British Columbia, so we are in the southern end of their range. Species are usually more prolific in the middle of their ranges than nearer the extremes, where conditions are not as favorable for them.

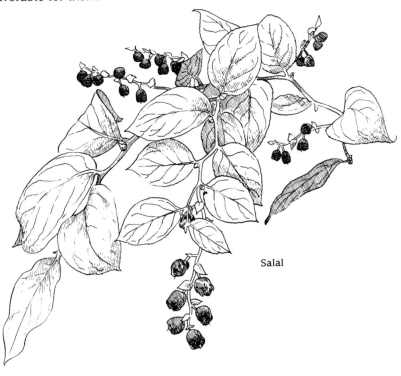

Salal

On the other hand, salal grows in numerous coastal parks. I have usually seen it in one of two habitats. In coastal scrub or on exposed hillsides it stays low to the ground and shows no trace of berries. In forests it is usually a couple of feet high; where the conditions are most favorable for it, the bushes top 5 feet.

Keep your eyes open for salal in wooded areas whenever you are on the ocean side of the coastal hills. For example, the plants grow on Mt. Tamalpais; in Point Reyes National Recreation Area and Tomales Bay State Park; on King Mountain on the Peninsula, though sparingly; and in Butano State Park. A couple of bushes produce a handful of berries on Mt. Davidson in San Francisco; with all its eucalyptus trees, it seems so altered by civilization that I was surprised to find these little native shrubs holding their own. Whenever and wherever your explorations lead you to some ripe salal berries, you will probably be surprised, too!

The berries generally ripen in mid- to late August.

Western Chokecherry (Prunus demissa, also P. virginiana var. demissa)

Western
Chokecherry

Chokecherry grows as a shrub or small tree, up to 15 feet tall, with smooth bark and deciduous leaves. The white flowers hang in clusters from April through June, followed by strings of sour, dark cherries in summer. The fruit is used to make fine jellies and syrups and was cherished by both Indians and pioneers throughout America.

Note: The cherry seeds contain hydrocyanic acid, related to cyanide, but cooking destroys it. Be sure to spit out the seeds if you eat the cherries raw.

While I have never heard of anyone confusing the two, you might want to compare this description and drawing to those of silktassel bush on page 19.

Where and When to Find It   The trick is finding chokecherries in this area; I still haven't. The shrub is rare in Marin. On the Peninsula it has been reported from Pilarcitos Canyon; Page Mill Road, near the summit; Permanente Creek; Coal Mine Ridge; and San Bruno Mountain. In San Francisco, it has historically been found near Lake Merced and on Twin Peaks, the San Miguel Hills, and the Bayview Hills. In the East Bay, it is rare on Mt. Diablo. It forms several groves in the Berkeley and Oakland hills, but the naturalist who spotted them has never seen any fruit on them.

   Chokecherry is found most often on wooded slopes or by springs or streams. It can also grow on brushy hillsides. When you are hiking in summer in a possible chokecherry habitat, keep an eye out for those strings of cherries, but don't set your heart on finding them.

Holly-leaf Cherry *(Prunus ilicifolia)*

   This small tree or large shrub falls in the category of "if you happen to come across it in fruit, it's nice to know that they're edible." The leaves are evergreen and hollylike. The fruits are dark purple with a large stone surrounded by a thin layer of sweet pulp.

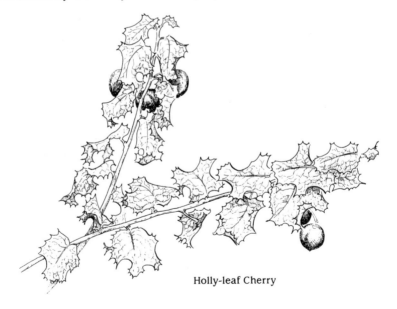

Holly-leaf Cherry

Where and When to Find It   I seem to be blind to this shrub, for I have yet to find it, even though it is supposed to be common on the Peninsula. Its favored habitats are chaparral, open hills, and ravines or gullies. Thomas (*Flora of the Santa Cruz Mountains*) reports it from San Francisco, San Bruno Mountain, Pilarcitos Dam, Menlo Park, Searsville, and Saratoga Summit, as well as areas further south. It grows on Bayview Heights above Candlestick Park and in the Montebello Open Space Preserve off Page Mill Road. In the East Bay, holly-leaf cherry is rare, and there are no reports of it in Marin. The shrub blooms in April and May, so look for the ripe fruits in July and August.

Pacific, Klamath, or Sierra Plum *(Prunus subcordata)*

Pacific plum grows here, but doesn't seem particularly content in doing so. The trees are rare in Marin and not common anywhere else in the Bay Area. Finding healthy, disease-free plums on them is a feat.

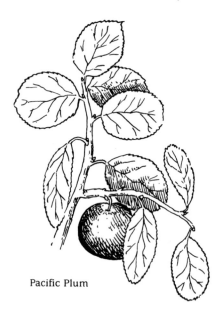

Pacific Plum

Where and When to Find It
The trees form small stands or thickets along creeks or in chaparral. In the East Bay, they grow on Mt. Diablo, in Briones Regional Park, and in the Berkeley/Hayward hills, especially above the Caldecott Tunnel. They also occur in the southern portion of the Peninsula, on the Bay side of the mountains; look for them at Portola, Coal Mine Ridge, Page Mill Road, and Permanente Creek. Pacific plum bears white blossoms in March and April, followed by mature plums in June or July.

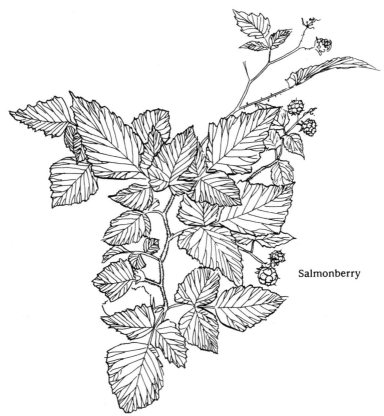

Salmonberry

Salmonberry *(Rubus spectabilis)*

Salmonberries are juicy and tart, so if you could find enough to cook with them, you could make something terrific. The Bay Area is near the southern end of their range, so they are not common here, but they do form some productive thickets along the coast.

They are easy to recognize. The leaves look like those of blackberries or raspberries, but the ripe fruits are golden orange or red, depending on the bush. The berries are made of small segments, like a blackberry, and a little bristle grows on each segment. Don't worry; the bristles are so soft and thin that you won't taste them.

Where and When to Find It   Salmonberries need wet soil and wet air, which they find on the ocean side of the Peninsula and Marin. A few of the places they grow include San Bruno Mountain, on the lower slopes of Colma Canyon; the western slope of Mt. Tamalpais; Tomales Bay State State Park; the Palomarin coast of Point Reyes National Seashore; and along the road between the Estero Trail and Johnson's Oyster Farm, also at Point Reyes.

Their blossoms are an unusual rose-pink and appear in March through May; the berries reach their prime in mid-June.

Red Huckleberry or Red Bilberry
(Vaccinium parvifolium)

This shrub grows from 2 to 15 feet high. Its leaves are smooth edged, small, and deciduous. The flowers and berries look like those of ever-green huckleberries, except that the berries turn bright red when ripe.

These berries are very tart and can be used, like cranberries, in a sauce. For every cup of berries, add a cup of sugar and just enough water to cover the bottom of the saucepan. Bring the mixture to a boil, stirring, and simmer it for 4 to 5 minutes.

Where and When to Find It   In the Bay Area, they grow only on the Peninsula and in northern Santa Cruz County. Even in those areas, red huckleberries are rare. They have been found along Pescadero, Butano, and Gazos creeks, and in Big Basin.

The shrubs bloom between March and June; look for the berries a few months later.

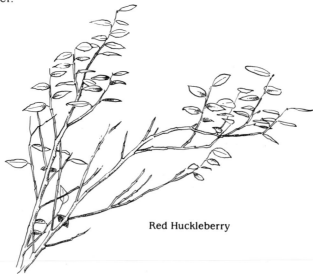

Red Huckleberry

NONPOISONOUS BERRIES THAT ARE BETTER LEFT TO OTHER ANIMALS

Each of the following plants held out the promise of foraging pleasure—and disappointed me. They are included here to spare you the same experience.

Coffee Berry *(Rhamnus californica)*

Coffee berry is not used as a coffee substitute, despite its name. None of the main foraging books or local experts treat it as an edible plant. The bark of its first cousin, another *Rhamnus* species that doesn't grow here, is a widely used natural laxative. Some settlers in this area saw the resemblance between the two species and used coffee berry bark as a substitute. But it is apparently inferior; contemporary guides to medicinal plants mention only the related species.

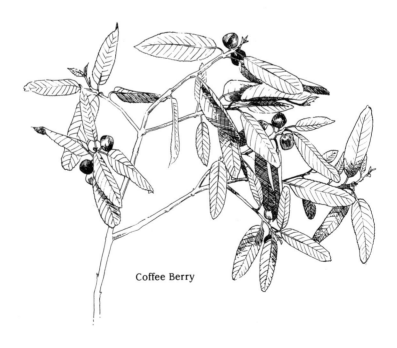

Coffee Berry

Twinberry

Osoberry *(Osmaronia cerasiformis)*
Twinberry *(Lonicera involucrata)*

Osoberries and twinberries are not poisonous, and foraging guides written for the Pacific Northwest speak highly of their flavors. But most of the berries produced in the Bay Area are impossibly bitter—the sort of bitter that leaves you spitting for a long time after a single taste. Is it something in the soil or the weather conditions here that alters their flavor so radically from what it is further north? California foraging guidebooks don't even mention these plants; if you taste them, you will find it hard to believe that people in Oregon and Washington are enthusiastic about them.

Toyon or Christmas Berry *(Heteromeles arbutifolia,* formerly *Photinia arbutifolia)*

This handsome native shrub with toothed, evergreen leaves bears beautiful red berries throughout the winter. Generations of California families have included toyon cuttings in their winter holiday decorating, with the special advantage that the berries can't hurt any toddler tempted by them. You will need to plant your own bush if you want to take cuttings; the local arboretums and native plant societies can give guidance on their nurture.

So far, so good. But the berries also have a reputation for tastiness that mystifies most people who try them. According to the history books, the Indians of Northern California relished toyon berries and ate a lot of them. Supposedly, the berries can be made into a cherry- and almond-flavored cider and are also good cooked. But my experiments with them have failed, and so have those of the other foragers I have asked. I hope that speaking honestly about this defeat will help others get over their private feelings of inadequacy caused by failure to produce anything tasty from toyon. Maybe the books are wrong or are omitting some critical piece of culinary or harvesting information.

The raw berries are bitter and astringent, but the lore holds that roasting or boiling them improves their flavor. One local ranger has experimented several times with baking them at 350° F. until they were soft but not burned; she says they lost some of their bitterness, but not enough to be enjoyable.

When I boiled them according to a toyon cider recipe, they lost their bitterness but not their astringency. The recipe said to boil them several minutes in an equal volume of water, puree the mixture in a blender, let it sit for an hour or two, and strain out the berry mash. The resulting cider was a lovely purple color, but it tasted like a puckery, unappealing cross between fruit and vegetables. Boiling it for a few more minutes with sugar did not improve it.

Perhaps the berries vary in flavor geographically, like twinberries and osoberries. The leaves seem to do so. Some have a wonderful cherry-almond fragrance when crushed, and I have found more of those in the Sierra foothills than here. In fact, I have only smelled that aroma from the leaves of one Bay Area bush. If the berries vary the same way, then maybe the Bay Area is just unusually bad toyon country. If you are ever able to make something tasty with toyon, please let me know.

I do love the bushes, despite the poor taste of the berries. The heavy clusters of scarlet berries are gorgeous against the green background of winter. The effect is especially dramatic in two parks where they are abundant: Wunderlich County Park on the Peninsula and Black Diamond Mines Park in the East Bay. But toyon is widespread and common throughout the Bay Area, so you can see it along many trails.

Note: Cotoneaster, a common garden shrub, could be confused with toyon, because its red berries are ripe in winter and its leaves are evergreen. However, the edges of cotoneaster leaves are smooth, whereas

Toyon Berry

those of toyon are coarsely toothed. Eating enough cotoneaster berries can produce cramps, diarrhea, and vomiting. I haven't heard that they taste good, so an adult probably wouldn't eat enough to get sick, but keep an eye on toddlers who may be attracted to the berries. And plant a toyon if you want a source of nontoxic cuttings for the holidays.

Where and When to Find It

Toyon needs some sun, so it grows in chaparral, grasslands, and open woods. "Open woods" means that you will find it among loosely spaced oak trees rather than in the deep shade of a Douglas fir or redwood forest.

A good deal of toyon is planted along freeways, and it seems to ripen there first. Usually by mid-October I see some ripe berries along Interstate 880, even though the ones in Briones Park, for example, are still yellow and orange. So if you do want to try your hand at cooking with them, don't be fooled into a premature harvesting trip by what you see along the highway.

By November the berries are red in most of the East Bay parks. Along the coast they normally redden by December. Many bushes retain their berries through January and February, while the last stragglers finally ripen.

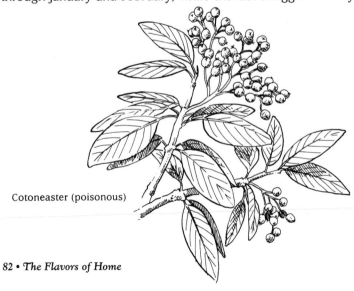

Cotoneaster (poisonous)

CHAPTER 5

Nuts

I n the Bay Area, as elsewhere, nuts ripen from mid-summer through the fall. Squirrels and acorn woodpeckers busily hide them away for winter feasting, while other animals simply eat their fill on the spot. You will have energetic competition for the best-tasting varieties. ❁ Unlike a berry, which is merely packaging for the seeds it contains, a nutmeat is meant to nourish the embryonic tree within it until the tree-to-be can extend a root into the soil and start getting food the adult way. When an animal eats a nut, a potential tree is destroyed. However, the reproductive strategy of a nut works anyway, because animals are sloppy and forget some of the nuts they so carefully tuck away. Because nuts taste good to animals and last long enough to be worth storing, they get carried to locations far from the parent tree. Some are buried in fertile soil and, through this dispersal system, oak or hazelnut habitats are gradually colonized. ❁ Unless you enjoy the labor of preparing acorns, the local nuts don't offer the sort of predictable pleasure to be found in wild berries and greens. But I enjoy scanning each hazelnut bush I pass in July and August, occasionally finding a nut or two the squirrels missed. You will find enough nuts to make you glad you have learned to recognize them.

California Hazel, Hazelnut, or Wild Filbert
(*Corylus cornuta* var. *californica*)

Hazelnuts, wild or domestic, have as rich a flavor as walnuts, without the walnuts' trace of bitterness. Their nutmeats are compact domes and are easily separated from their shells. They are, in short, great nuts.

Hazel shrubs in forests are open rather than compact; in autumn their yellow leaves form a loose pattern of yellow dots against the dark background of the trees, rather than a solid mass of color. The leaves have toothed edges and feel slightly fuzzy. The nuts usually grow in pairs, but can be clustered in threes or fours. Each nut is covered with a fuzzy, papery sheath that wraps around it and tapers to a long tail.

Ripe nuts have brown sheaths; immature ones are greenish. The sheaths are often covered with tiny, fine bristles that can stick to your fingers, so gloves are a help. Or just wrap any corner of clothing around them when you pull them off a bush. It's easy to pull the sheath off. Inside you will find a nut that is smaller but otherwise identical to the hazelnuts sold in stores.

Where and When to Find It   Finding hazelnuts is partly easy, partly hard. Hazel bushes are common here, particularly on moist slopes (especially with northern exposures) and in canyons. They grow on brushy slopes, as on San Bruno Mountain, and in woods both dense and open. While you can easily find them in Marin, on the Peninsula, and in the Berkeley/ Hayward hills, they become less

California Hazel

frequent to the east, where the climate is hotter and drier. As far east as Mt. Diablo, hazel bushes become rare.

The hard part is finding the nuts, because the squirrels gather so many. However, they do miss a few, so it's worth scanning the bushes you pass. To realize how many they eat, go to the one Bay Area location that has no squirrels: Angel Island. There the hazelnuts ripen undisturbed, and the abundance of nuts hanging from most twigs is a truly satisfying sight.

While occasional nuts mature by June or even May, July and August are the main months to harvest them.

Golden Chinquapin *(Castanopsis chrysophylla)*

Golden chinquapins are handsome trees that are related to the domesticated chestnut. Unlike chestnuts, chinquapin nuts are tiny, but they are tasty. Unfortunately, humans are not the only creatures who think so, and though a tree's nut production is great, it's a challenge to get to any of them before the competition does.

You will be able to identify the trees easily enough. The leaves look much like bay leaves on top, but their undersides are distinctly yellow or gold. The rounded casings for the nuts are covered with spines so long and sharp that they are probably the Bay Area's most intimidating harvest.

The ripe casings split open just enough so that you can see whether any nuts are inside. Use gloves to pick any thorn balls that look promising. At home, you will want pliers or similar tools to pull them apart. Inside will be a few nuts measuring about ⅛ by ¼ inch down to ⅛ by ⅛ inch. Inside those tiny shells are the nutmeats, if you are lucky. A good number will be mildewed, already eaten by tiny creatures, or dried to a crumbly dust. One determined forager brought home two full bags of casings and got only fifty to sixty decent nutmeats from them, about four tablespoons' worth.

So what's the point of the whole experience? Well, before I tried a golden chinquapin harvest, those trees meant little to me. They were just part of the backdrop in most hikes along coastal ridges. But now, whenever I see their thorny hulls, I get a jolt of pleasure. I enjoy knowing that I can eat what's inside the casings if I want to. And there's an even greater delight in knowing that I never have to harvest them again.

Golden Chinquapin

Where and When to Find It   These trees grow on ridges among chaparral plants and are much more common in the coastal counties than in the East Bay. Some of the places you can find them in Marin are on Mt. Tamalpais, on Bolinas Ridge, and on Inverness Ridge in Point Reyes. A typical location on the Peninsula, with many trees, is along the Ridge Fire Road in Butano State Park.

Time is of the essence in gathering the nuts. They ripen in September and early October, and the weevils are ready for them. So look for them by late September; if you wait until mid-October, as I did once, you can miss the entire harvest.

California Black Oak *(Quercus kelloggii)*
Coast Live Oak *(Q. agrifolia)*
Tanoak or Tan Bark Oak *(Lithocarpus densiflora)*
Valley Oak or California White Oak *(Q. lobata)*

Oaks so often look enchanted here. In the coastal forests, live oaks draped in wispy lichen thrust powerful limbs into twisted, gnarly arcs that sometimes touch the ground, creating a domed space for dreaming. In open grassland, lone oaks spread their branches wide and give the landscape a center, a presence, that captures our hearts. From coastal woods across warm valleys to the Sierra foothills, the oaks are a constant, the symbolic essence of native California.

Deciduous oaks such as the black oak and valley oak are especially lovely in spring. Their leaves emerge tiny, perfectly formed, and red, like newborns after their first breaths. The new foliage is so red that it looks more like blossoms than leaves; a grove of oaks in fresh leaf is every bit as beautiful as the flowers that grow beneath the trees.

People miss some of the comfort to be found in oaks if they do not realize how great a role these trees have played in the nurturing of humankind. Any mature oak tree, in addition to lifting your spirits with

Valley Oak

its strong, sheltering form or tender new leaves, could provide your daily bread and keep you alive.

Acorns are known to have been a food of the Persians, the Japanese, the early Greeks and Italians, the prehistoric Swiss Lake Dwellers, and especially the Spanish, whose oaks grew sweet acorns that did not require extensive leaching. Writers Susan Alvarez and David Peri unearthed a delicious quote to the effect that in Madrid, acorns were such a popular snack that ladies constantly ate them at the opera.

Perhaps the people most profoundly bound up with the oaks have been the California Indians. Until recently, acorns were their main staple, the staff of their lives. The journal *News from Native California* quoted two Pomo Indian women who captured the centrality of the oak tree's role:

> In our language, we call the tanoak *chishkale;* it means "The Beautiful Tree." It's beautiful to look at. I never get tired of seeing it; it always lifts up my heart and makes me feel good. Every time when I go about the country to doctor the people who calls me to them, that tree, when I see it for the first time, lets me know I'm home, and I feel good. . . . It's like a relative or good friend. It may sound funny to the white people, but that tree is beautiful because it gives us good food too and it's sweet too; I'm always happy when it's acorn picking time; I don't know how to explain it better than that.
>
> Long ago it was our most common food; we ate it every day. We stored up as much as we could. We still gather up those acorns now. Sometimes the people has hard times, no jobs, no work, but that tree still feeds us; sometimes it's the only food we have to eat. I guess that's why the people in olden days gave that tree this name, beautiful.
>
> —THE LATE ESSIE PARRISH, RELIGIOUS LEADER

> The Indians and the acorn trees is just like the same thing. We wouldn't be the same Indians if there wasn't acorns.
>
> —ELSIE ALLEN

Each phase of acorn gathering and preparation had a rich tradition. The Indians gathered the acorns in the fall, as a group event. Then the nuts were stored in rain-proof containers that also kept out interested animals. Dried acorns can keep for years without rotting because the tannin in them acts as a preservative. Throughout the year, the women pounded the nutmeats, leached out the bitter tannin, and cooked the acorn meal into breads, soups, and porridges. Whenever I see the smooth, rounded depressions in large boulders, often alongside streams, marking the places where women sat together hour after sun-dappled hour, pounding acorns and laughing and swapping stories, I am wistful at the contrast with our isolated modern lives.

V. K. Chesnut, who interviewed Northern California Indians years ago, learned that some oaks were more desirable than others. Tan bark oak acorns needed a lot of leaching, but were considered the best because of their pleasant acid taste and oil-rich meat. California black oak acorns come second; though they were not plentiful, the acorns were so rich in oil that they were excellent for breads or soups. Valley oaks grew so large and had such big acorns that they produced the most abundant harvests and thus were a major source of acorns. Blue oak acorns were

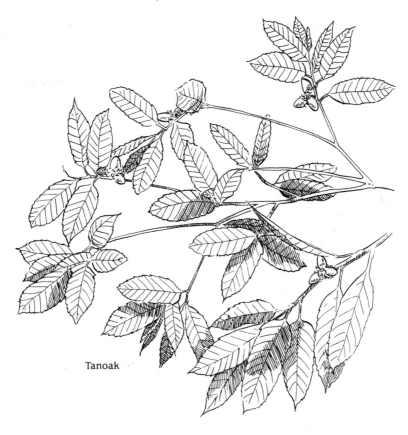

Tanoak

California Black Oak

eaten, but canyon live oaks were usually inaccessible and their acorns required so much leaching that they were seldom used.

If you want to taste the mush that fed Californians for thousands of years, here are some tips. For more detailed information, refer to *It Will Live Forever: Traditional Yosemite Miwok Acorn Preparation* by Bev Ortiz (Berkeley, CA: Heyday Books, 1990).

There is an art to the harvest. The best time to gather acorns is usually the second half of September through early October, but it varies a little each year. The acorns fall off in two stages. The first group to fall tends to be buggy. The second round is the one you want.

After you have removed the outer shells, it is important to dry the kernels sufficiently so that the red husks surrounding them can be rubbed off. They are bitter.

All local acorns are inedible until the tannin has been leached out of them. After grinding or crushing the acorn meats to a coarse meal (or to a floury texture if you want bread), you can leach it by wrapping it in cheesecloth and tying the cheesecloth around a faucet so that water can drip through the nuts. Leave the tap on at a dripping rate overnight, or however long the acorns require. When the leaching is finished, there should be no noticeable bitterness left.

Now you have a food ready to be cooked. Simmer the meal in more or less water, and you get soup or porridge accordingly. I found the plain meal utterly bland, in part because it was so waterlogged. However, it proved to be a malleable food that could take on real character if given a chance.

My greatest acorn success was this recipe: Finely chop a garlic clove or two, and stir over low heat in oil or butter until the garlic turns golden. Add the leached, damp acorn meal (presumably you will have about a cup, unless you have been particularly industrious). Stir the meal and

Coast Live Oak

garlic over medium heat for about 10 minutes to evaporate the water and to cook the meal. Keep the mixture gently simmering. When it develops a savory taste, add salt and freshly ground pepper and eat it.

This porridge was delicious. It tasted like mashed, seasoned beans, and gave me the contentment of knowing that, at least once in my life, I had been able to appreciate the food that an oak tree provides.

Where and When to Find Them

California Black Oaks   As a member of the Red Oak family, this is the only oak in the Bay Area that has deeply and irregularly lobed deciduous leaves with sharply pointed tips. The trees grow in the developed valleys around the base of Mt. Tamalpais and on the hills of the Peninsula, particularly to the east of the main crest. In the East Bay, they are most common in Briones Park and in the hills in the Orinda/Lafayette area, but they also grow in Las Trampas Park, the Morgan Territory, and on Mt. Diablo.

Coast Live Oaks grow as far inland as Mt. Diablo, despite their name. These are the trees that assume such fantastic, twisted shapes in the woods, along with the canyon and interior live oaks, which also grow here. You will see them growing with bay laurel trees, often near streams, on hillsides, and in valleys throughout the Bay Area. Their leaves stay green all year long, and are small, with pointed edges that curve downward.

Tanoaks or Tan Bark Oaks are coastal trees with evergreen leaves. They are common on the Peninsula and grow on Mt. Tam, Bolinas Ridge, and Inverness Ridge in Point Reyes. Look for them at the edges of redwood forests, among madrones and bay trees. Unlike live oaks, tanoaks have long, narrow leaves that feel slightly fuzzy on the undersides.

Valley Oaks or California White Oaks   Like all white oaks, these trees produce acorns whose meat is far less bitter and requires less leaching than that of live oaks or red oaks. The deciduous valley oak leaves are deeply lobed, like the black oaks, but the lobes have rounded rather than pointed edges. Their acorns are particularly long.

On the Peninsula and in Marin, they grow in the valleys and the low hills east of the Coast Range. In the East Bay, they grow east of the Berkeley/Hayward hills. For example, they are found at Briones, Las Trampas, and Sunol parks, on Mt. Diablo, and in Walnut Creek and the San Ramon Valley.

The new oak leaves were at their best on one walk I took in Wunderlich County Park in late March. In early May, they were still small and red at Castle Rock State Park, but were already green in Sunol. Even in Sunol, though, they were still noticeably smaller than mature leaves, and added much to the tender, spring feeling in the air.

The best acorn harvest is normally in early October.

Walnut *(Juglans hindsii)*

This native walnut was originally found in only three locations, each of which had been an Indian community: Walnut Creek; Wooden Valley east of Napa; and along the banks of the Sacramento River, especially at Walnut Grove. Three small areas and nowhere else on earth.

Since then, they have spread along riverbanks throughout agricultural areas in Northern California. Their numbers have grown because of their usefulness to orchardists. Being native, they have a greater resistance to the local insects and fungal diseases than do English walnuts; so all the English walnut trees grown here are grafted onto Hinds walnut rootstocks. If untended, the rootstocks will send out branches of their own, bearing the native walnuts.

When you try to crack open your first native walnut, you will understand why they aren't grown commercially. The shells are much thicker than those of English walnuts. Our nutcracker is inadequate for the task; the one time I tackled some native nuts, I ended up hammering them out on the back steps.

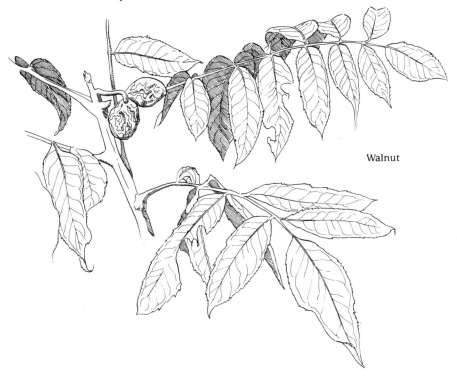

Walnut

Where and When to Find It You will find these trees in the East Bay, rather than in Marin or on the Peninsula. The town of Walnut Creek is an obvious place to begin. Moraga has many walnut trees along its public trails, as does Briones Park, in the old orchard on Orchard Trail. The trees also grow along Pinole Creek, Alhambra Creek, San Pablo Creek, Coyote Creek, Alameda Creek, Calaveras Road, and in Niles Canyon.

The nuts ripen in October and the leaves turn yellow then, as well.

See also
California Bay Nuts, page 199

CHAPTER 6

Greens and Other Vegetables

When I was a child and visited my grandmother in Washington, D.C., we would walk all over the city together. One year, she discovered a patch of lamb's quarters growing on the sidewalk at the edge of a construction site. Whatever exhibit we had been to that day is a faded memory, but not so the adventure of picking the leaves together and having them for supper that night. ❀ Having lived through the deprivations of World War I in Europe, she had a highly developed sense of thrift, which the weed satisfied. Having spent my childhood in the heyday of stable, suburban prosperity, I had a highly developed craving for the exotica of a peasant lifestyle. We were quite a team, contentedly squatting down on the sidewalk to choose the best-looking leaves. ❀ That was my introduction to urban foraging. These days, I'm pickier about harvesting sites and would avoid taking leaves from a spot so near the street, with its lead fumes. Maybe by the time I'm a grandmother, life will have loosened me up and I'll have an "oh, why not" attitude about locations again. ✿ Fortunately for middle-generation, rigidly health-conscious Bay Area folk, even our cities offer plenty of appealing foraging sites. My favorite weed picking has been in San Francisco. I love to remember a cool, grey January day when I gathered a meal's worth of wild radish and mustard greens at a site overlooking the Golden Gate Bridge. Whenever I stood up to stretch, I could watch the gulls circle the fishing boats clustered over the herring schooled in the Bay. ✿ One joy of foraging for weeds and other greens is that so many grow close to home, wherever home may be. If you live in the suburbs, you may have a good selection in your own yard. If you live in an apartment, the nearest urban open space is likely to be well supplied, especially given the meager funds alloted for park maintenance. The weedy greens thrive on disturbed soil conditions, which is why they have a bad reputation: they flourish best where we want them least—in the disturbed soils of gardens, lawns, and croplands.

Miner's Lettuce *(Montia perfoliata)*

Soon after my husband and I moved to the Bay Area, we noticed an odd plant unlike anything we had seen in the East. It was about 6 inches tall, and each stem growing out of the ground had one flat, circular leaf at the top of it. The leaf was like a dish, turned up to the sky. A little stalk of tiny, white flowers grew out of the center of the leaf. The mystery plant grew in great numbers under the eucalyptus trees where we liked to walk. Some of the stems in these colonies had a single, triangular leaf on them, with no blossoms. We asked friends about it, but none of them were botanically minded and no one knew its name.

A year later, we saw a notice for a lecture and slide show on Indian uses of local native plants. We thought it would be fun to know something about the edible plants here, so we went. Suddenly, there was our

Miner's Lettuce

mystery species up on the screen. Its name was miner's lettuce, and we learned that it had been eaten by both miners and Indians.

The next time we went up to the eucalyptus woods, we each ate a leaf. That was a very special moment. It was our first opportunity to reach down and taste the California landscape directly.

As we hiked on weekends, we had been absorbing the sounds, fragrances, and vistas of the countryside. We were falling deeply in love with the Bay Area. Now we had taken a step toward knowing this land with all of our senses. Eventually, the taste and feel of many local plants would become familiar, all because we had enjoyed our first nibble of that oddly circular, smooth, little leaf.

Miner's lettuce is one of the best species for a beginning forager to learn about. It is easy to identify, tastes familiar and pleasant, grows abundantly in city parks and remote woods, and is fresh and tender for at least six months of the year. It is a bread-and-butter plant for foragers. There is nothing exotic about the taste, but when you feel a need to nibble on a wild food or to bring a harvest home from the outdoors, finding miner's lettuce is an easy and satisfying way to do so.

The flavor and texture of miner's lettuce are virtually indistinguishable from any of the tender, loose-leaf lettuces. It is so likable and "normal" tasting that it was one of the few California native species taken back to Europe to be cultivated as a regular crop. (We occasionally serve miner's lettuce at parties. One time, not a single guest noticed that the salad wasn't standard supermarket fare. And they were a fairly sober, observant bunch. Clearly, for some friends, it is worth spending the time to pick wild greens, while for others, equally dear, store-bought foods will suffice.)

Apparently, some of the California Indian tribes had an extraordinary way of adding flavor to their salads made of this plant. Ants leave a trail of formic acid on the ground as they walk, so that they can follow the trail back to their anthill. The Indians spread miner's lettuce leaves around the entrances to anthills, and the ants' acid trails across the leaves gave them a tang much like the vinegar or lemon juice we add to our salads.

Many foragers have a special fondness for miner's lettuce unrelated to its taste. It serves as a much-anticipated herald of the new growing season. All during September and October I wait for it. The ground beneath the trees in our favorite forests is so dull. The herbs and grasses that were strawlike in early summer have faded by fall to a greyish tan, one of the deader colors. When the scattered autumn rains have finally soaked the soil enough for those odd little leaves to appear, they fill me with a sense of fresh beginnings.

Miner's Lettuce

Many wild greens start growing in autumn: chickweed, fennel, and radish, to name a few. Why does miner's lettuce seem so special? Perhaps because it is a California native and the other outstanding edible greens are not. Miner's lettuce was signaling the start of the growing cycle long before the other species arrived. Tasting it taps you into a line of California rainy seasons going back thousands of years. Because it is native, it can be found in truly wild places, whereas introduced greens generally grow where there has been some human disturbance. Yet unlike most natives, miner's lettuce grows as abundantly as many weed species, massing in healthy drifts over large areas of a forest floor.

We also love it for its quirky, spunky shape. Miner's lettuce looks like some sort of affectionate joke, like a cartoon that manages to say something interesting about life and be funny and tender as well.

Where and When to Find It   Locating miner's lettuce is relatively simple because it thrives throughout this area. People can find it near their homes even in cities; it thrives in quiet urban spots, tucked away from the heavy traffic of feet or cars. If you prefer to taste plants from wilder, cleaner woods, you can find it in such places as well, far from the nearest asphalt. It is unusually broad in its distribution, growing well on Mt. Diablo and in the radically different climate and environment of San Francisco's parks.

The common element in all good miner's lettuce spots is moist shade. It grows best under trees. I have seen large patches under eucalyptus, Monterey cypress, oaks, and a palm tree. However, I don't recall finding it in bay laurel or redwood groves. Typical of spots where it flourishes are the eucalyptus groves in the Presidio in San Francisco, in Tilden Park, and on San Bruno Mountain; in Wunderlich County Park on the Peninsula; and in the grassy oak woodlands of the East Bay. A grove is not necessary; a lone tree can support a healthy colony of miner's lettuce at its base.

The plant will also grow on sunny, trailside slopes, but in such places the leaves turn reddish and stay very small. Once you recognize the plant, you will almost certainly be able to find a patch of it near your home, wherever you live in the Bay Area.

The season for gathering miner's lettuce is longer than that of almost any other seasonal plant in the Bay Area. The leaves appear within a few weeks of the first hard rain of autumn and are ready to eat from then until the rains end in the spring. In a wet year, miner's lettuce covers the ground by mid-October, whereas in drier years you may have to wait for it until late November.

At first, you will see more of the triangular leaves. As the winter progresses, the circular leaves become dominant. Both taste equally good. By February or March, most of the round leaves have sprouted spires of little white flowers. You can eat the flowers and stem, too, if you wish. Unlike many edible species, miner's lettuce does not turn bitter once it blooms. In a year of long and heavy rains, the lettuce will stay green and tender through April, and sometimes beyond. Most years, though, the leaves in my favorite patches are faded and uninviting by mid-April.

Asparagus *(Asparagus officinalis)*

Don't get your hopes up too high. Wild asparagus is an unusual sight in the Bay Area. Still, it does grow here, and what passionate forager would not be willing to go the extra mile for this, the most sought-after of wild vegetables.

A man who lives near Suisun Marsh described the location of one patch to me, and I went searching for it in the warm light of late afternoon at the end of March. The marsh was lush with fennel, hemlock, and radish, except for still-flooded areas that reflected the sky. Birds sang everywhere.

I walked slowly, scanning the ground. Suddenly, there it was, unmistakable among all the more common wild things. Until that moment, finding wild asparagus had always seemed the sort of event that might happen to a Euell Gibbons, but not to anyone that I knew. We all harbor quiet yearnings for certain experiences. This had long been one of mine.

This asparagus was king sized, clearly thriving on the brackish water and rich but loose soil of the marsh. Several stalks stood 2 feet tall, one or two supporting themselves by twisting around a handy branch. Height and width seemed unrelated; some tall ones were thick, others thin. Even though they were so large, their heads were still tightly closed, a sign that the stalks would be tender.

Did you know that if you break off a growing asparagus stalk, its juice may run all over your fingers? These stalks were full of sap and tasted like store-bought asparagus, only fresher. But flavor was only part of the thrill in that heady moment on the levee.

Near these monster asparagus, I found more dark purple heads just barely poking above the ground. Some things concentrate the essence of a season so powerfully that they flood us with the emotions we attach to that time of year. These vigorous, dark, pushing plants *were* spring, as acutely as a nest full of eggs or a tree misted with tiny leaves.

How wonderful it would be to live near enough to walk the levee at dusk each day in late winter, watching for that first asparagus tip. As a child in Tennessee, I used to search for the first daffodil shoots in that way, pawing through the dry leaves where they grew. Winter was rich with daily suspense and a sense of private treasure.

If you do find this particular asparagus patch, please content yourself with only a few spears. It is a small clump—enough to supply two or three families or a steady trickle of honorable visitors. On the rare occasions that asparagus is given a chance to mature and go to seed, it grows

Asparagus

into a tall, feathery form that remains as an attractive dried weed until the next spring. The red berries are pretty but poisonous. The old stalks look noticeably different from the dried shoots of fennel or hemlock, which are abundant along the levees.

Even if you don't find asparagus, the search for it will lead you to spend a few hours in special country. In Suisun Marsh, you can rest your eyes on the long vistas and distant hills that define this big-sky region. A thousand birds will sing in your hearing, and the coot pairs will make you smile with their energetic escapes on the sloughs and marshes as you approach. Egrets and herons will fly by or stand poised against the lush greens and clear blues of the land and water. You can breathe hours of gentle spring air. After such a morning or afternoon, you are likely to come home feeling very lucky and alive, no matter what success you have had in your asparagus hunt.

Where and When to Find It The Delta area is well suited for this vegetable, which needs sun and moist soil. Asparagus is grown there commercially. As a result, if you wander the Delta levees, you have a chance of finding the occasional clumps of spears that have escaped from cultivation.

Some levees are closed to the public; but on Grizzly Island, a state refuge in Suisun Marsh, people are welcome to roam during the springtime. While I have promised not to be specific, I can tell you that there are at least two vigorous clumps of asparagus somewhere on the Grizzly Island levees.

Browns Island near Pittsburg is reachable only by boat, but it is part of the East Bay Regional Park District and also supports a healthy asparagus population. I have not heard or read of asparagus growing wild anywhere else in the Bay Area.

The spears are ready for eating in March and early April.

Bracken Fern *(Pteridium aquilinum)*

Gathering fern fiddleheads in spring is a rite so classic that even *Gourmet* magazine carries articles on the subject. Before bracken ferns

Bracken Fern

unfold, the small, coiled tops can taste like almonds. They are used raw in salads, steamed, or baked in casseroles. When cooked, the best ones develop a delightful flavor that's a cross between nuts and mushrooms.

Any immature fern frond, still curled, is called a fiddlehead. Most species actually look like the coil carved into the top of a fiddle. Bracken ferns are branched at maturity, so their fiddleheads have several coils at the top of the stem, rather than just one. This makes them easy to recognize.

While all fern fiddleheads are edible, some contain more bitter tannin than others. Bracken ferns are among the least bitter and the most common, two good reasons to confine your foraging to that species.

Each fiddlehead is like one leaf on a plant. It is connected underground to a number of other fern fronds, all of which nourish their common root system. So if you gather this vegetable, don't pick all the fiddleheads in one place. Move around, so that each root system will be left with enough fronds to gather sunlight and keep the plant alive.

Note: only collect those ferns which are still tightly coiled. As they begin to uncurl and spread their leaves, they become terribly bitter, and *mature leaves of every species are poisonous.*

I have found that about one in three bracken fern fiddleheads are somewhat bitter, while the others are quite good. However, some fields seem to produce a higher proportion of bitter ones. It is a good idea to taste a few raw ones before gathering in a new spot, to make sure you like them. In any case, the bitterness increases further down the stems, so only harvest the coiled tips and at most the top 1 inch of stem. The bitterness can be reduced by soaking the fiddleheads in water for 24 hours or cooking them in several changes of water, but it won't disappear.

Now for the bad news. A high consumption of bracken fern fiddleheads has been linked to esophageal cancer, so this is not a food to eat frequently. In fact, in January 1990, bracken fern was added to the official state list of substances known to cause cancer. People have been celebrating springtime with a dish of fiddleheads for a long time, so it is hard to imagine that total abstinence is necessary for longevity. However, I have to admit that seeing bracken fern on the Proposition 65 list, sandwiched between the likes of bis(chloromethyl)ether and bromodichloromethane, has largely taken away my appetite for these almondy morsels.

Where and When to Find It   Bracken ferns are among the easiest foraging greens to find because they grow in grasslands where their large size and distinctive shape are conspicuous. A particularly good time to locate the plants is in November and December. The grass is short and green then, whereas the dried, mature ferns are a coppery brown.

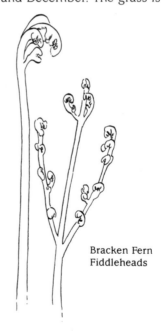

While the most typical habitats for bracken ferns are grasslands and brushy slopes, they also grow in open oak stands or woodlands. This fern is common and widespread throughout the Bay Area, although more so in the western than the eastern portions of the East Bay counties. One spot where they are particularly abundant is in the Marin Municipal Water District lands, where they have aggressively invaded the grassy areas. The fiddlehead season is in March and April.

Bracken Fern
Fiddleheads

Cattail *(Typhaceae latifolia, T. angustifolia,* and others)

Euell Gibbons described cattails as "the supermarket of the swamps" because of the unusual variety of foodstuffs one can get from them. The uses made of this single plant bear testimony to the resourcefulness of our species, particularly when hungry.

Some cattails are attached to an underwater stem, running horizontally between plants. That stem, when peeled down to the starchy core and whirled in a blender with some water, can be sieved to remove the fibers. What's left is water containing a flour that will settle to the bottom of the container. You can pour off most of the water, dry the flour, and use it in combination with other flours for baked goods.

Where mature cattail stalks intersect the horizontal underwater stems, you will find a walnut-sized ball of starch that can be used like a potato. Off those same underwater stems come pointed, curving shoots that will be the next year's plants. These can be peeled and steamed as vegetables. If you grab a cattail plant just inside the outermost leaves and pull straight up, the whole stalk will come up. The bottom portion of it, when trimmed of roots and peeled, can be eaten raw (for a cucumber flavor) or steamed (for a cabbage flavor).

Finally, the new cattail heads, when they are still green and wrapped in papery sheaths, can be peeled, steamed or boiled for a few minutes, buttered and salted, and eaten like corn on the cob. When these bloom spikes are slightly more mature, the sheaths come off and the spikes are covered with yellow pollen that can be collected and used in baked goods.

There. I felt it was my duty to say all that, because every foraging book I have ever seen waxes so enthusiastic about the endlessly useful and delicious cattail. So the odds are good that you may have an equally good time trying all these things.

However, I have become a fan only of the pollen. A cattail plant is a strong, deep green, vital thing. Whenever I have pulled or dug one up, and stood there, holding a plant as tall as myself for the sake of a walnut-sized potato and an equal amount of cucumber/cabbage, I have wanted to cry.

It's not that the cattail population is particularly hurt by such foraging; in some marshes, such as at Coyote Hills, the cattails must be periodically thinned. Once established, the species is tenacious.

But, in most cases, harvesting a cattail makes me feel like I have lost a round in the foraging game. The food value gained seems too small

Cattails

and ordinary compared to the handsome vigor of the plant that is traded for it.

Using the still-green cattail heads as vegetables does not have such associated problems, and the cooked immature bud material tastes pleasant enough. But the edible portion is only about ⅛ or ¹⁄₁₆ of an inch thick, around an inedible core. After I have buttered, salted, and scraped the stuff off with my teeth, I'm left feeling that this may be valuable as a one-time exercise in learning about cattails, but it doesn't qualify as an experience to be sought out each year.

Gathering the pollen is an entirely different matter. Harvesting is a pleasure, the preparation is simple, and the pollen has attributes that can't be bought in stores.

My husband and I went to a marsh late on a weekend afternoon toward the end of May in pursuit of pollen. Euell Gibbons wrote that one could easily gather several pounds' worth in a few minutes, but we were late in the season (for that year; it can vary considerably). We saw few under-ripe bloom spikes and many that had already lost their pollen to the winds. It took about 40 minutes of walking around the marsh, shaking every remotely yellow spike, to gather ⅔ of a cup between us.

The pollen is a clear lemon yellow. It is simple to collect it by bending each yellow-dusted cattail head into a plastic bag and shaking it by the stem. Hold the bag closed with your other hand, and a minimum of pollen will be lost to the air. Some cattail fluff will shake off into the bag along with the pollen. Don't worry about it; it is easily sieved out. The pollen itself is as fine grained as talcum powder.

By the next morning, several small insects and a spider had crawled out of the pollen and were high in the plastic bag. We poured everything into a sieve, and then liberated the bugs out the kitchen window along with the fluff. You may need to sift the pollen several times to remove all the fluff.

We used our pollen to make pancakes, mixing it half and half with whole-wheat flour. They were delicious and an attractive brownish yellow color. From all reports, pollen can be used in most baked goods in a 50:50 ratio with another flour.

That's my idea of a fine foraging food. Cattail pollen is versatile and probably very nutritious. It gives food a beautiful color and a rich flavor. Best of all, gathering it is an excuse to linger in a marsh in May, when the sun is setting and everything is shining, golden, and green.

Where and When to Find It   To uproot plants, you definitely need to talk first with a ranger or avoid parklands altogether. For example, at Coyote Hills Regional Park, the park naturalists will tell you if any thinning needs to be done and, if so, where. Grizzly Island is another place with some accessible cattail stands, and rangers are always in attendance to advise visitors. Calling these places before you go will lessen the chance of being disappointed.

Gathering pollen can be done at more places than these. Probably the best description of cattail distribution in the Bay Area would be: widespread and occasional. They grow throughout the region in a great variety of watery habitats, including ditches, slow portions or backwaters of streams, coastal or bay marshes, and the edges of lakes. On the other hand, they are not a particularly common sight. Since cattail spikes are so conspicuous, you can easily spot them if any are in your area.

Harvest times vary considerably depending on how long the rainy season lasts in a given year. The cucumber/cabbage-flavored shoots are available sometime between February and May. The underwater spurs have a similar but slightly longer season. The green corncobs or flowering heads appear between late March and May, and the heads develop ripe pollen between May and July. The roots are available for harvesting the year round.

Chickweed *(Stellaria media)*

There are three species whose leaves I wait for, longingly, in the last months of the dry season: miner's lettuce, dock, and chickweed. They are delightful in their own right, but time spent harvesting them is also time to savor a world reawakened by rain. Winter's arrival soothes and refreshes like cool water on a tired face. Every surface sparkles in the clear, washed air. On the hill near our home, the eucalyptus leaves rustle overhead and scent breezes already fragrant with damp earth. It doesn't take long to pick enough stems for a salad; the entire slope is covered with them. All is soft, green, and moist, and will be so for months to come.

Any chickweed not used in salad the day it is picked will be good in sandwiches the day after. The leaves are so delicate and bland that cooking them seems like overkill, but some people like them slightly steamed. Raw, they are a splendid cross between lettuce and sprouts. A chickweed salad is an attractive, airy tangle of slender stems and petite leaves. Try tossing the stems in a vinaigrette with thin slices of scallion, green peppers, and mushrooms.

Chickweed got its name because young chickens eat it avidly. It's the right size for chicks; it has such weak stems that the plants stay low. They grow in dense clumps and have tiny white flowers. When you look closely at the stems, you will see tiny hairs along them, but you won't taste those.

Scarlet pimpernel looks similar, but has red flowers and hairless stems. Since eating large quantities of scarlet pimpernel can be bad for you, you may want to wait until the chickweed is blooming before you harvest it the first year. After that, you will be able to tell them apart by the more subtle cues of stem and leaf texture.

Caution: watch for poison hemlock (see page 17) in the chickweed patches. The two species thrive in similar habitats, so it is common to

Chickweed

find them growing together. The young hemlock plants are about as tall as chickweed in late fall, and it is *important* not to mix any in with your salad by mistake. Usually, if hemlock has infested one area, you only need to move a few yards away to find a patch that's solid chickweed. Move those few yards. If you can't feel carefree about the harvest, then lettuce and sprouts are a better deal.

Where and When to Find It   Chickweed grows throughout the Bay Area, in moist, lightly disturbed soils. These would include yards, urban and suburban parklands, fields, and grazed grasslands. This introduced species has become very common.

The plants appear within a few weeks of the first hard rains in fall; usually by late October they are readily available. They grow more lush as the rainy season progresses, peaking from January through March. By late April, most chickweed starts to fade and is overshadowed by taller species.

Chicory *(Cichorium intybus)*

The best evidence indicates that chicory came to California along with the influx of settlers in 1849 and the 1850s. It is known for its bright blue flowers that close in midday when the sun is shining. The roots of this attractive weed, if sliced, roasted dark brown, and ground into a powder, can be used just like ground coffee beans. In fact, chicory coffee appears on menus in New Orleans.

Chicory leaves are edible when very young, but they become quite bitter as they mature. They are only good for a short time after they appear, well before the plant flowers. Experienced chicory foragers recommend digging into the soil deep enough to cut off the top of the root, with the leaves attached, since the underground portion of the leaves is the best part.

Chicory

The plant can be grown without sunlight long enough to produce a cluster of blanched leaves. Since it is sunlight that makes the leaves bitter, some people grow chicory under cans or in basements to assure themselves of a crop of this green. I have only seen chicory when it was too mature to eat, so I cannot vouch for the flavor of its leaves. However, the young ones must be delicate and tasty if they can inspire people to engage in basement farming.

Where and When to Find It

To see chicory in bloom and learn to recognize the species, go to Meadow Road at Point Pinole Regional Shoreline. There chicory grows up to 30 inches tall and is in flower from June to November. Once you have seen mature plants, you can go to the same place early in the spring and learn to identify it in its edible phase.

Throughout the Bay Area, the simplest way to find this hardy plant is to watch for the blue flowers in summer and fall along quiet roads, in vacant lots, or on grassy hillsides. Chicory is not listed in *The Flora of San Francisco*, but does grow in numerous towns in Marin, in the East Bay flatlands, and in the Santa Clara valley.

Once you have found a convenient clump of the plants, you will need to check the site periodically in late winter and spring, until the leaves appear.

Curly Dock *(Rumex crispus)*

Whenever the autumn rains begin in earnest, be it October or November, dock responds quickly, sending up a rosette of long, narrow, wavy-edged leaves. These are among the finest wild greens available. Chopped coarsely and steamed briefly, they combine the rich flavor of spinach with a hint of lemony tartness and are very high in vitamins A and C.

Enjoy the leaves while the rainy season lasts. By May, most of the plants will have developed tall, central stalks, and at that point the leaves become bitter. Confine your harvesting to those plants which are still simple rosettes.

Regarding identification: let the seed stalks of the previous year guide you to the plant. Dock's seed stalks stand several feet tall, with a thick cluster of rust-red seeds at the top. They are an attractive feature in the autumn and winter landscape, and, until the rains beat them down, you

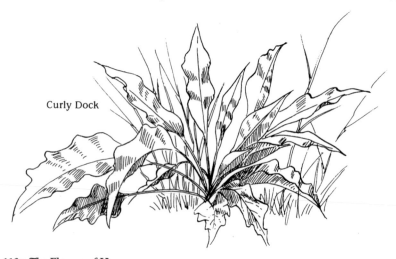

Curly Dock

can make use of the fact that new leaves will appear at their base. There will be many rosettes with no seed stalks, but all seed stalks will stand near rosettes.

Another point to keep in mind is that certain wild evening primroses also grow in rosettes and have similar leaves. It will be easy to tell them apart if you remember that primroses have a red vein down the center of each leaf (red being the color of flowers), whereas dock leaves have green veins (green being the color of vegetables). If the leaves don't have a lemony flavor, spit them out. You have got the wrong plant.

One of dock's many charms is that its leaves are large enough to make harvesting easy. You can gather enough for a meal very quickly.

Mature Curly Dock

Where and When to Find It

Dock needs a lot of water. It grows in the rainy season in wet places, such as the edges of streams, marshes, drainage ditches, low fields, ponds, and irrigated lawns. You may have it in your backyard. The most I ever saw in one place was out on the Grizzly Island levees in Suisun Marsh, but I can find plenty in the weedy areas of the city parks near our home. This introduced weed is virtually indestructible, so eat all you want. You will find it throughout the Bay Area, wherever there is the right degree of sunlight, moisture, and human influence.

The first plants to appear in the fall will be too mature to eat by midwinter, but lots of others will have put out leaves by then. Eat your fill between October and April; when I have found young dock in the summer, it hasn't tasted as good as the winter leaves.

Sweet Fennel *(Foeniculum vulgare)*

People who liked licorice as kids usually like fennel as adults. If you didn't like licorice, maybe you should skip this section.

Fennel was brought here from the Mediterranean and has since become a common weed throughout this area. Its seeds, leaves, and stems are basic to many French and Italian recipes.

This species is easy to recognize. Fennel grows to be a bushy plant about 5 feet tall. The leaves are soft and needle fine, like dill weed, so that from a distance the plant has a fuzzy, indistinct outline. Crushing the leaves, stems, or seeds releases a distinct smell akin to anise and licorice. The large, flat, yellow flowers are followed by fat, green seeds that turn brown and hard as they dry.

Fresh stems and leaves develop beginning in late January. While the stems are half an inch or less in width, they can be used as raw vegetables, eaten with dips or spread with cottage cheese. Later, they become too fibrous.

Fennel stems can be substituted for celery in many recipes. Chopped fresh leaves are used to season fish, salads, soups, or potatoes. They lose their flavor if dried.

TOMATO, CARROT, AND FENNEL CASSEROLE

Cook until tender:
- 1 cup chopped onion
- ½ cup chopped green pepper
- 3 tablespoons oil

Add:
- 1½ cups thinly sliced carrots
- 1½ cups fennel stems, cut into ½-inch lengths
- ½ teaspoon salt
- dash of pepper
- one 8-ounce can tomato sauce
- ¼ cup water

Heat the mixture to boiling and put it in a one-quart casserole. Cover the casserole and bake it in a 400° F. oven for about 1 hour. Serves four to six.

Sweet Fennel

The green seeds appear in late summer and fall. They are chewy and delicious eaten plain. Both green and dried, they are used in apple pies, cookies, cakes, fish or meat dishes, and with vegetables. Fennel seed tea is fragrant and satisfying.

A few plants produce nearly flavorless seeds; if the ones you find are disappointing, don't think they are typical. *A note of caution:* one time I saw a poison hemlock growing interspersed with a fennel bush. The two plants were the same height and were setting seed at the same time, and the scraggly hemlock was almost invisible in the midst of the voluptuous fennel bush. This sort of hidden boobytrap is uncommon and should not keep you from exploring fennel's delights. But if you chew some fennel seeds and taste nothing, why not spit them out, just in case. Hemlock seeds are flavorless.

Where and When to Find It   Fennel is common and widespread in disturbed areas of Marin, San Francisco, and the Peninsula. In the East Bay, it is common in the communities nearest the Bay, becoming less so inland. Vast quantities grow at Coyote Hills Regional Park and in Suisun Marsh. Because this plant grows so tall and often dominates vacant lots, it is one of the easiest edible weeds to locate.

Harvesting times vary between locations, as always. In the most favorable areas, the first fennel shoots appear as early as November, but the majority of plants develop in February and March. This is the time to try the stems. The leaves are good throughout most of the year, as long as you can find fresh, green ones. Fennel blooms between May and October. By August, the green seeds are on the plants at Suisun Marsh. By October, the plants along Panoramic Highway in Marin are full of them. Most of the dried seeds are beaten off of the bushes by winter rains, but wherever fennel grows in abundance, you can often find a seedhead still full of seeds as late as March of the following year.

Garden Orache *(Atriplex hortensis)*
Fat Hen *(A. patula var. hastata)*

Both of these *Atriplex* species have edible, nutritious leaves that can be eaten raw but are better steamed. The leaves are distinctly triangular. Sometimes they have a slightly bitter aftertaste, but their dominant flavors are good. The leaves become meltingly tender with a few minutes of cooking.

Where and When to Find Them   Garden orache grows in the East Bay as a weed in people's gardens and in disturbed places and salt marshes on the Peninsula.

Fat hen is common in salt marshes and on the flats adjacent to them. It grows along both the Bay and the coast in Marin and from San Francisco southward. Great quantities of it also grow a mile or two out on the levees at Grizzly Island in Suisun Marsh.

Both species have an extremely long season because they continue to produce new leaves throughout the year. The fat hen on Grizzly Island was up and attractive by February one year, while some harvested along the Bay was still quite tasty in August.

Fat
Hen

Garden
Orache

Green Amaranth or Rough Pigweed
(Amaranthus retroflexus)

The tender, young leaves and tips of amaranth, if picked when only a few inches high, are said to have a mild, bland flavor. The tiny but super-abundant black seeds are supposed to be good when roasted about an hour in a medium oven. I haven't yet come across this plant, so I can only pass on to you other people's recommendations.

Amaranth stirred up a lot of interest in the 1970s and early '80s. I remember seeing an entire book devoted to it once in a health foods store. Conferences were held to discuss its potential as a food plant. Both the seeds and the leaves are highly nutritious, and for a time it was thought to be a potential miracle food for malnourished populations. In China and elsewhere, it is grown as a crop.

In America, however, most people still treat it as a weed. Based on when its seeds started appearing in the adobe bricks of old buildings, scientists think green amaranth most likely arrived in California between 1825 and 1848. It has been invading gardens ever since. If you have been pulling it out of your yard, you might try steaming the next crop of leaves and eating them with butter and lemon.

Where and When to Find It *Amaranthus retroflexus* is said to be fairly common on the Peninsula, occasional in the East Bay, and rare in Marin.

Unlike most local, wild greens, which shoot up during the rainy season, amaranth needs the warmth of summer to grow. While it can be found along roadsides and in vacant lots, it thrives best in the places that get summer water: gardens.

The easiest time to locate amaranth is when it is full grown, in summer and fall. The plants produce green flowers in the second half of the summer, followed by seeds in late summer and early fall. The young leaves are at the harvesting stage in this area in May and early June.

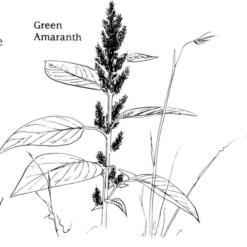

Green Amaranth

Lamb's Quarters or White Goosefoot
(Chenopodium album)

When I ate lamb's quarter leaves as a child back East, I remember them as tasting just great, steamed and seasoned with butter and salt. Even though lamb's quarters does grow in the Bay Area, I haven't yet noticed it here, and so cannot give you an updated evaluation. But the leaves loom large in foraging literature across the country; some authors surmise that more people eat lamb's quarters than any other weed in the United States. (Maybe a good question for the census, long form, would be, "What weeds do you consume?" Then, when the tally was in, books like this could say, "It must taste good; 36 million Americans can't be wrong.")

Lamb's quarters arrived in California sometime between 1769 and 1824, during the period of Spanish colonization. Its almost triangular leaves are shaped somewhat like a goose's feet, giving rise to its other common name. The goose's toes are formed by the indentations in the leaf edge. The leaves are mealy looking, dark green on top and grey-green underneath, with a whitish green vein down the center. Mature plants can grow to be several feet tall, with an upright, central stem.

Lamb's Quarters

The young leaves are used cooked or raw and are a richer source of Vitamin A than spinach. After the plants flower, the blossoms mature into dry clusters at the end of every branch, clusters that contain the tiny, dark seeds. The seeds can be ground and used in porridges or baked goods. To harvest them, strip the clusters into a pail, rub them between your hands to loosen the seeds, and winnow off the husks. Even though the seeds are tiny, numerous foraging books insist that they are produced in such great quantity that it is fairly easy to collect usable amounts.

Where and When to Find It   Lamb's quarters grows in disturbed ground. This includes roadsides, fields, grazing lands, vineyards, and waste ground in towns. In Marin and the East Bay, where it is most often found in pastures, lamb's quarters is said to be widespread but not common. The Peninsula supposedly has more of it.

The leaves should be gathered when the plants are young and tender, so look for them in the spring. Lamb's quarters blooms from July through October and sets seeds thereafter.

Prickly Lettuce *(Lactuca serriola)*
Wild Lettuce *(L. virosa)*

These two species are challenging. On the one hand, they are readily available here, are tender additions to salads, and have other pleasing properties. On the other hand, their leaves must be eaten when very young because they rapidly turn bitter; and in that young stage, they lack the distinctiveness of shape that would make them easy to recognize.

Fortunately, the Tilden Nature Center sponsors a salad walk in late winter, on which the naturalist identifies both types of lettuce and picks their leaves for the big salad served back at the center. That's the best way I know to learn to recognize these species.

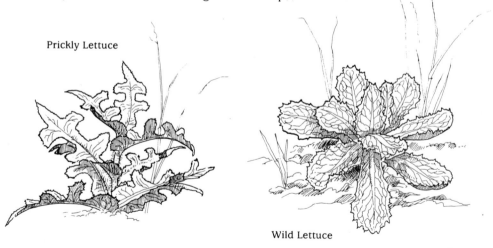

Prickly Lettuce

Wild Lettuce

These lettuces contain sedative, calming chemicals in sufficient concentrations to be listed in the *U.S. Pharmacopoeia.* While you are unlikely to notice any effects from eating them in salad quantities, the lightly steamed leaves reduce in volume so much that you may eat quite a few. Some people feel a pleasant languor after a generous portion of the cooked greens.

If you like these lettuces enough to want to extend their brief season, you can freeze them for cooking later.

Where and When to Find Them   Prickly lettuce is a common weed of roadsides, pastures, cultivated fields, and other disturbed ground throughout the Bay Area. Wild lettuce is most common in the Oakland and Berkeley hills, tapering off to occasional status elsewhere in the Bay Area.

Harvest the leaves in January and February. You may want to locate the plants in late spring and summer, when they grow quite tall, so that you will know where to find them the following winter.

Mallow or Cheeseweed *(Malva* species*)*

Mallow leaves are so rich in Vitamin A that it could actually be unhealthy to eat a large helping every day. However, an occasional serving would do most of us a lot of good.

The mallows come in many sizes in the Bay Area. Some are low garden weeds; others grow to 4 feet tall with thick stalks. In each case, the leaves have a distinctive, rounded shape. Most are slightly fuzzy, especially the leaves of the taller species. The five-petaled flowers are pinkish, veined with deep red or purple. The seeds that follow them are large, often thumbnail sized, and in a papery casing. Peeling the casing back reveals a pale green ball shaped like a wheel of cheese.

The cheeses, as the seeds are called, are bland, but pleasant enough for nibbling. I always pick at least one when I pass a mature mallow. To eat them raw, remove the husk. However, the cheeses can also be cooked and used like peas, and for cooking you can leave the husks on.

The leaves keep a slight fuzziness even when cooked, but this can be masked by chopping and mixing them in casseroles or stir-fries, or serving them with cheese sauces. It is worth experimenting to find a mallow recipe you enjoy, because the leaves are flavorful, without any bitterness.

Mallow

Mallows have a long and far-flung history in human affairs. The ancient Mediterranean peoples celebrated the leaves' ability to restore health to the weak. The Chinese appreciated them in fine cuisine. The original marshmallows were made with an extract from the roots of the marsh-mallow, *Althea officinalis.*

Unfortunately, marsh-mallows do not grow in this area, though they have become naturalized in the East. I've read that the roots of our local mallows can be boiled with figs to make a cough syrup. Euell Gibbons wrote that boiling a cup of unpeeled cheeses in 2 cups of water until the water reduced to 1 cup would produce a liquid similar to that from true marsh-mallow roots. His approach sounds both easier and less destructive, since you don't have to uproot the plants. He recommended combining the mallow liquid in equal parts with honey and orange juice as a remedy for coughs and throat irritations.

Where and When to Find It   Mallows are common throughout the Bay Area in all the usual weed locations: roadsides, fields, gardens, and any other disturbed or waste ground. The biggest mallows I have seen grow at the edge of the dirt parking lot above the Sutro Baths and the Cliff House in San Francisco. They are as stout as little trees!

Soon after the autumn rains begin, young mallows appear. It is easy to find tender, new leaves from November through February. The plants bloom from March through October, and the cheeses are available from April through November. The location of the mallows affect harvest times: plants in warm areas dry up during the summer, whereas along the coast they get enough moisture to bloom and bear through the fall.

Dwarf Nettle *(Urtica urems)*
Hoary Nettle *(U. holosericea)*

Nettles are familiar to most people as the source of a painful, tempo-
rary rash when touched. The new leaves and shoots of young plants
under a foot tall are also a vitamin-rich, tender vegetable when cooked.
If you want to try them, wear gloves to gather them. Fifteen minutes of
simmering is more than adequate to destroy their stinging qualities,
and they are good in soups or stews. It is worth being conservative about
cooking time; undercooked, they can swell the tissues of your mouth
and throat and cause real misery.

The plants have an unbranched main stem. The leaves are roughly
heart shaped with long, pointed tips and are toothed all the way around
their edges. The whole plant is covered with tiny, stinging hairs containing formic acid, which is the culprit. (Isn't it odd that the same formic
acid, when left as an ant trail across miner's lettuce leaves, is a valued
flavoring rather than an irritant? Why the difference?)

Curly dock (see page 110) often grows near nettles, since the two have
similar habitat requirements, and dock leaves rubbed on a nettle sting
are supposed to take away the discomfort. Something in the juice of
fresh leaves is said to interact chemically with the formic acid to neutral-
ize it. I have also heard that one is supposed to chant "Dock in, nettle
out" while rubbing. All I can say is that this hasn't worked for me. I
deliberately brushed against nettles repeatedly one time so that I could
test the dock theory, and no amount of vigorous rubbing with juicy dock
leaves seemed to make the slightest difference, with or without chanting.

Where and When to Find Them   Nettles grow in wet, rich soil.
Hoary nettle is found in natural settings, such as along streams in redwood forests, whereas dwarf nettle (said to have the best flavor) grows in
gardens and waste places. Clumps of willows indicate potential nettle
habitat. These species are occasional but widespread in the Bay Area.

Dwarf nettle blooms in March through June, hoary nettle in May
through October. Since the leaves must be collected before the plants
bloom (after which the leaves become tough and gritty), the harvest
months are roughly from February through the summer, depending on
the species and location.

Hoary Nettle

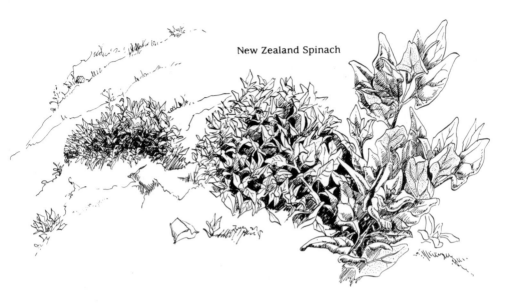

New Zealand Spinach

New Zealand Spinach *(Tetragonia tetragoniodes)*

If you like to experiment with the various green, leafy vegetables for sale, then you have probably tasted New Zealand spinach. It is usually marketed in clear plastic bags, stuffed full of the leaves.

Exactly the same plant grows wild here along the Pacific coast and the Bay shore. Native to Japan, New Zealand, and other parts of the western Pacific Rim, this species has migrated to coastlines around the world, including ours.

New Zealand spinach grows in clumps several feet across, so it is relatively easy to spot. The leaves are thicker than average, dark green, and sparkle a little, as though salt crystals had dried on them. If you eat one before washing it, you will taste the saltiness of the ocean air in which this plant thrives.

This is one of the few leafy vegetables that is in season all year. A plant will have some harvestable leaves on it in any month. The leaves are good to eat as long as they are solid green. When they begin to fade or turn brown, they are past their prime. To do the least harm to the plant, pinch off the mature leaves rather than pulling them, so that the main stalks won't be damaged.

Many foragers simply steam the leaves and flavor them with butter and salt or a sauce. I prefer to use them in soup. Try simmering them in chicken broth for 1 to 3 minutes (just long enough to wilt them), alone or with any other vegetables or flavorings you like. The leaves absorb the chicken flavor and their fleshiness makes a satisfying contrast with the clear broth.

Where and When to Find It   New Zealand spinach usually grows within sight of saltwater but beyond the reach of waves. In an area with cliffs above the ocean, it will sometimes grow on the headlands at the top of the cliffs. In other words, you will find it in the vicinity of a shoreline but substantially back from the water's edge.

Along the San Francisco Bay shoreline, I've seen it at Candlestick Park. Neil Havlik has seen it on beaches between the Bay Bridge and Point Pinole, and *The Flora of San Bruno Mountain* reports it from Point San Bruno and Brisbane Lagoon. You will undoubtedly find it elsewhere as well, if you explore the Bay shoreline.

In San Francisco, I've seen it along the headlands under the Golden Gate Bridge, on the shore of Lobos Creek behind Baker Beach, in Lincoln Park, and in large clumps just north of Thornton State Beach. *The Flora of San Francisco* reports it at some of the same places, plus Golden Gate Park, Lake Merced, the Potrero and Bayview hills, Islais Creek, and Hunter's Point.

In Marin, I've seen it at Rodeo Lagoon at Ft. Cronkhite, at Tennessee Cove, on the headlands between the Point Reyes lighthouse and Chimney Rock, and at McClure's Beach. *Marin Flora* also lists it at Lime Point, Angel Island, San Rafael, Stinson Beach, and Dillon Beach.

Along the San Mateo coastline, I have only seen it at Pescadero Marsh. You will surely find it behind other beaches, if you look.

As this partial listing indicates, there is no shortage of places to find New Zealand spinach. You will probably choose to get most of your spinach from a store, saving both your time and the coastal vegetation. But seeing a familiar vegetable growing wild is all the more satisfying if we normally buy or cultivate it. How often do we come upon such clear links between our ordinary routines and life in the wild?

Pickleweed *(Salicornia virginica)*

Some edible wild plants are hard to find. Not pickleweed. You will find lush stands of it at virtually every marsh that borders bay or ocean waters in this area. In winter and early spring, the plants stay brown even though the surrounding hills are covered in fresh grass. Then in April and May, pickleweed comes into its own. The new growth appears, rejuvenating the marshes with fresh green. Just about the time that your favorite leafy spring greens are becoming too mature to be tasty, the prime season for pickleweed foraging begins.

Pickleweed looks unusual, so it is easy to identify. Each plant consists of round, branching stems that are divided by joints into individual segments. The leaves and flowers are so tiny that you will probably never notice them. The plants look simple, tidy, and primitive.

This plant's story is bittersweet. A salt marsh is a difficult environment; such concentrations of salt would kill most land plants. Pickleweed dominates large areas of marsh here and on other continents because its succulent tissues can store up water in the spring, when rain runoff reduces the saltiness of the marsh. The plant then uses that stored, relatively fresh water through the summer growing season. Its tissues can also withstand an internal salt level that is much higher than most species could bear (whereas some other salt-marsh species have special mechanisms for excreting the salt). So, at first glance, the plant appears to be a standard ecological success story: adapt to a unique niche and thrive.

The truth is more poignant. Scientists who grew some pickleweed in soil dryer than its normal marsh setting found that it grew faster and better than normal. And the less salty the water they gave it, the more it thrived. It appears that pickleweed would "love" to be a normal dry-land plant, but something in its makeup renders it unable to compete with dry-land species. So it survived by adapting to a hostile setting that its competitors could not tolerate. The cost of the adaptation is that individual plants never grow as luxuriantly as they could if pickleweed had evolved a way to compete directly with the rain-watered land species.

The science of plant ecology is still so young and primitive that we are unaccustomed to feeling tenderness for the hardships of plants, for the drama of their lost potential. For most plant species, we don't yet have a clue about the nature of those hardships and trade-offs. As we learn more about other species' mechanisms for survival, surely some of the false distance and sentimentality that many feel toward the plant

Salt Marsh (Pickleweed in Background)

kingdom will ebb, replaced by greater intimacy and identification.

What do you do with a harvest of these odd-looking, jointed stems? Refrigerate it in an airtight bag or container, just as you would any green vegetable. It will stay fresh for three weeks or longer. I ignored some in my refrigerator that long and it tasted fine when I finally got up the courage to prepare it.

Eaten by itself, raw, it is too salty for my taste, even when it is well washed. However, pickleweed can contribute attractive looks and refined flavor to a salad. My husband and I ate it with lettuce, avocado, scallions, tomatoes, and fresh raw peas. Like the peas, it was slightly bitter and slightly sweet. The pickleweed also tasted a bit sour. We didn't add any salt to the oil and vinegar dressing, since pickleweed contains so much. That way, its saltiness was not a problem and, in fact, tasted good in combination with all the other vegetables.

As you have probably guessed from its name, pickleweed is good pickled as well as fresh. It has been gathered for that purpose from the marshes of northern Europe for centuries. Most of the pickleweed pickle recipes given in books are similar to each other. The recipe given here is a modified version. If you decide to use an entirely different pickling recipe, adapted for cucumbers and the like, skip the brining step. Pickleweed amply reflects its own briny origins.

Making these pickles is fun and simple. And they are pretty! A wedge of ordinary cucumber pickle looks dull compared with the delicate, branching shape of pickleweed and its clear, dark green color. As for flavor, pickleweed pickles taste much like any sweet pickles. The pickle-weed's own flavor is completely masked by the pleasing combination of pickling spices, vinegar, onion, and sugar. You can alter the flavor to your taste by reducing or omitting the sugar or by adding bay leaves or other seasonings.

Gathering pickleweed is satisfying in part because you can snap each piece off neatly at a joint, leaving little trace of your action. Because the stems snap off so easily, walking through a stand of pickleweed leaves an ugly trail of broken plants. If you harvest from the edge of a patch, your work can be invisible.

This plant really is a delight. If you make pickles in the spring, they'll be ready in time for all the salads, sandwiches, and elegant cold dishes of summer. And come June and July, if you itch to bring home some wild green tidbit, pickleweed will be one of the few still in its prime. That's a great time to head for a marsh and savor its lushness, within sight of the tawny, dry hills.

Where and When to Find It

The best time to gather pickleweed is from April through July, although you may find the tips green and succulent earlier or later, depending on the marsh. For example, at Grizzly Island, large areas are kept flooded until late in the spring. The new year's growth tends not to develop until May. However, the pickleweed in those fields will still be lushly green through August, whereas the stands in less-managed marshes will be drying out by mid-July.

In autumn, pickleweed has more to offer your eyes than your tastebuds. As it dries, it takes on new tones, coloring the marshes with broad sweeps of deep red and purple.

Pickleweed

PICKLEWEED PICKLE

Have ready clean half-pint glass jars. I use the ones with coated metal lids and metal screw rims. Half-pint-sized pickles are perfect for sandwiches; if you want even longer pickles, you can double the ingredients and use pint jars just as well.

For every half pint of pickles, mix together:
- 1¼ cups vinegar
- 2 tablespoons sugar
- ¼ onion, sliced
- 2⅓ teaspoons whole pickling spices (you can buy them already mixed)

Boil the mixture for 10 minutes. Meanwhile, wash the pickleweed, and wash and rinse your jars, lids, and rims very well. Just before the 10 minutes are up, rinse the jars in hot water and pack the pickleweed into them so that the leaves stand vertically. Pour the vinegar mixture boiling hot over the pickleweed, filling the jars to the rim. Immediately put on the metal lids and screw them down tightly.

When the jars have cooled, test them for a vacuum by pressing on the lids. If the lids do not give under your fingers, the jars are vacuum sealed. Store them for at least three weeks in a dry place out of direct sunlight, and then the pickles will be ready to eat. Try them on open-face sandwiches, since their shape and color are so attractive.

If the metal lid clicks down and up as you press and release it, the vacuum did not form and the pickles will spoil if left on a shelf. (A vacuum denies bacteria the oxygen they need to decompose food.) Put that jar in the refrigerator. You can still enjoy that batch in salads, especially in seafood or chicken salad.

Making pickles is one of the most relaxing types of canning because the dread botulinus toxin can't grow in such strongly acid foods. Some people like to dilute the vinegar in pickle recipes with water to make a milder pickle. That's fine, but *take care that at least half of the pickling liquid is always vinegar.* As long as the mixture is at least 50 percent vinegar, it will be completely safe.

Pickleweed grows in most, if not all, of the brackish or salt-water marshes around the Bay Area. In the North Bay, you will find it at Rodeo Lagoon (Ft. Cronkhite, GGNRA), Bolinas Lagoon, Indian Beach (Tomales

Bay State Park), China Camp State Park, Pickleweed Park (San Rafael), Muzzi Marsh (Corte Madera), Bothin Marsh (Mill Valley), Tubbs Island (San Pablo Bay National Wildlife Refuge), the Napa marshes, and Grizzly Island Wildlife Area. In the East Bay, look for it at the Martinez, Point Pinole, and Hayward Regional Shoreline parks, the Emeryville mud flats, and the Elsie Roemer Bird Sanctuary. On the Peninsula, try the Palo Alto Baylands, San Francisco Bay National Wildlife Refuge (near Alviso), and Pescadero Marsh.

Some of these marshes are small, heavily visited, and thus not good places to forage. Some may be too polluted. Others are clean enough and well able to spare some pickleweed stems. Use your judgment and follow the posted regulations or talk with a ranger. You can enjoy pickleweed's beautiful autumn colors in any of these spots.

Purslane or Purselane *(Portulaca oleracea)*

It's odd to call purslane a weed, since it is raised as a vegetable in India. Indeed, it is such a respectable plant that *Joy of Cooking* includes a recipe for cream of purslane soup. However, because it grows in gardens unbidden, most purslane goes unappreciated here.

This species is low and sprawling, with fleshy, smooth leaves somewhat like those on a jade plant. Its flowers are small and yellow. The fresh leaves and stem tips are eaten raw in salads. They can also be boiled for a few minutes, sautéed, added to casseroles and soups, or pickled. The next time you weed some out of your garden, consider taking it to the kitchen to experiment a bit.

Purslane

Where and When to Find It   Gardens and orchards are the places to look for this plant. The most I ever saw was in Brentwood at a U-pick orchard. It was abundant between the rows of peach trees. Purslane is said to be common on the Peninsula, occasional in Marin, and widespread in the East Bay. Wherever you live, begin by checking your garden or those of your friends. You can harvest the leaves throughout the spring, summer, and fall.

Sea Rocket *(Cakile maritima, C. edentula)*

Sea rocket, a member of the Mustard family, is a fairly common plant on beaches and dunes along the Pacific coast and the East Bay shoreline. The tender, crisp leaves and stems are good raw in salads or sandwiches, if you enjoy a sharp, powerful horseradish flavor.

Sea Rocket

Cooked, they lose much of their pungency, and are a pleasant enough, mild green vegetable.

The leaves are deeply lobed, so that the leaf edges curve in almost to the central vein before curving out again. Look for a low-lying, succulent plant with the small, four-petaled flowers characteristic of the mustards. The blossoms range in color from pink to purple.

Sea rocket has been involved in an unusual environmental intrigue. Between 1880 and 1882, *Cakile edentula* arrived in the Bay Area. Botanists think it came in the wet ballast of a ship from the East Coast, where it is a native. It spread rapidly in this area and soon was abundant in scattered locations.

In 1935, botanists spotted *C. maritima* at Stinson Beach, the first sighting of this species in the Bay Area. This *Cakile* is native to the Mediterranean but has spread all over the world. Since then, the later arrival has almost completely displaced the earlier one in this area.

It is not altogether clear why one has displaced the other so quickly and so thoroughly. One theory is that it is because *C. maritima* produces more seeds. Or possibly some predator or parasite prefers *C. edentula*. *Cakile edentula* looks similar to *C. maritima*, except that the waves or lobes along its leaf margins are much shallower, staying farther out from the central vein. By 1970, botanists thought it no longer grew in

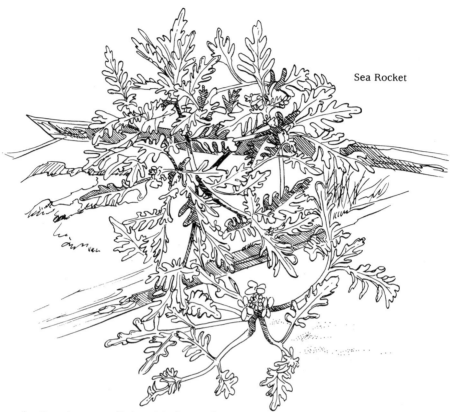

Sea Rocket

the Bay Area at all, but it's fun to keep an eye out for it, just in case you spot an enclave they have overlooked.

Where and When to Find It   Howell (*Marin Flora*) records *C. maritima* from almost every Marin County beach, from Angel Island up to the Point Reyes Peninsula.

Thomas (*The Flora of the Santa Cruz Mountains*) mentions "disturbed areas near San Francisco Bay," as well as San Francisco, Half Moon Bay, and Pescadero.

Botanist Neil Havlik has seen it fairly commonly around the South Bay and on the East Bay shoreline as far as the Carquinez Bridge.

In San Francisco, I have seen it along the Golden Gate promenade (between Ft. Point and the Marina Green), near the Sutro Baths in Lincoln Park, and at Ft. Funston.

Unlike so many wild greens, which become bitter when they flower, sea rocket stays tasty all year. Since it blooms from at least April through October, the flowers are usually available to help with its identification.

Sheep Sorrel *(Rumex acetosella)*

Sheep sorrel is a pretty plant, making low clusters of narrow, fish-shaped leaves. In late spring, its red seedheads contribute as much color to the grasslands as most meadow flowers.

The leaves are tender and sour, and can be used in any recipe calling for domestic sorrel. Since the wild leaves are not as tart as the cultivated ones, you will need to increase the quantity to get the same flavor.

Sorrel is classically used to make cream of sorrel soup or a green sauce for fish, but sheep sorrel is also good in salads or sandwiches. If you cook the leaves two or three minutes in very little water and then blenderize them, the resulting sorrel puree is delicious added to other soups. My favorite mixture is cream of asparagus soup with pieces of chicken and just enough of the puree to add a zesty tartness.

Sheep Sorrel

Sheep
Sorrel

Where and When to Find It

Sheep sorrel grows in grassy, open settings. Look for it on headlands, on grassy hillsides and meadows, in pastures, and at the edges of golf courses. Like so many introduced species, it is now common and widespread throughout the Bay Area.

Where the plants receive extra water from frequent fog or irrigation, they will produce leaves throughout the year; but in most places, this is a plant to harvest in the winter and spring. It is uneven in its development. I have seen abundant fresh leaves in San Francisco in November, whereas plants at Tennessee Cove in the Marin headlands were just beginning to grow in mid-February. In March, sheep sorrel is in its prime throughout this region. The seed stalks appear in April and May.

Watercress *(Nasturtium officinale,* formerly *Rorippa nasturtium-aquaticum)*

Watercress has a tony reputation, thanks to its use by British aristocracy in watercress sandwiches and by French chefs in cream of watercress soup. But, being common and widespread and a rare source of winter vitamins, this plant has been far more important than a mere ingredient in haute cuisine. For thousands of years, watercress has been appreciated by people in Europe and Asia for its power in pulling children and sick adults through difficult winters. The colonists regarded it highly enough to bring it to America. Since it spreads extremely easily, it can now be found in springs and slow-moving creeks throughout this country.

The secret to watercress's year-round availability is its characteristic of growing in springs. The earth beneath the top, insulating layers of soil does not change temperature through the year, even in areas of extreme weather patterns. So spring water, which flows from deep in the earth, comes out at a fairly constant temperature. As a result, watercress can continue to grow through much of the winter, even in areas where the cold is harsh. In the Bay Area, where most greens die off in the summer and fall for lack of rain, watercress keeps going strong, due to its wet feet.

Unfortunately, watercress will absorb harmful bacteria into its leaves if the streams in which it grows are polluted. If you cook the cress, that's not a problem; boiling kills germs in plants just as it kills those in water. So you can always use wild watercress in soups, as long as it is allowed to simmer awhile.

To use the leaves raw, in salads or sandwiches, either gather them from water that you know to be pure (no cows upstream, no leaking septic tanks nearby, etc.), or use water-purifying tablets. The tablets are available at most pharmacies or back-packing stores. Dissolve one in clean water, following the directions given. Let the watercress soak in the water for as much time as the instructions require for ordinary water purification.

Any comprehensive cookbook will contain several watercress recipes, so making use of your harvest will be no problem. I like the pungent, peppery leaves tossed with avocado slices, peas, and a vinaigrette dressing. As soon as you get home, rinse the leaves and seal them in a plastic bag or stand them in a container in a little water. Either way, they will stay fresh in the refrigerator for at least several days.

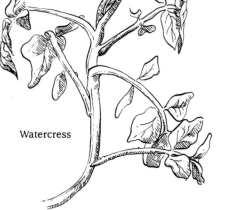

Watercress

Where and When to Find It

Watercress grows all over the Bay Area, from seeps and creeks in San Francisco to the springs of

Watercress

Mt. Diablo. It is widespread and common wherever a spring trickles out of a hillside or a stream is both slow and shallow (a good watercress stream is usually 1 to 6 inches deep).

One of the joys of this plant is that you can find it when other wild greens are scarce, in the dry months. It is also abundant throughout the rainy season.

GREENS I HAVE GIVEN UP TRYING TO LIKE

All of the following plants are not only edible, but in some cases are highly recommended in other foraging books. Maybe they taste different elsewhere. If you want to be thorough about tasting your way through the Bay Area landscape, you will need to try these and come to your own conclusions. Otherwise, I suggest you spare yourself.

Dandelion *(Taraxacum officinale)*

I've had no luck with dandelions; all the hints in foraging books on how to make them palatable have failed in our kitchen. Perhaps they need colder winters to develop the right flavor. Or perhaps other foraging authors have a higher tolerance for bitter foods than I do.

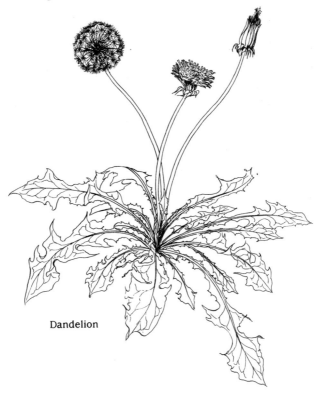

Dandelion

Since they are such a famous foraging item, you may want to experiment. The basic focus of every dandelion recipe is on ways to reduce or avoid the bitterness. Only use plants that have not yet bloomed. For salad greens, the least bitter portion is the white part of the leaves below the soil surface. The green portion of the leaves makes a tender, vitamin-rich, cooked green, but must be boiled in several changes of water. The roots can be roasted in a low oven until dark brown throughout, then ground and used as a coffee substitute. The flower buds still hidden down in the crowns are boiled as a vegetable.

Where and When to Find It   The best place to look for dandelions is in yards or urban parks. They are most common in rich soils near human dwellings. In the East Bay, they are more common near the Bay than in the interior; they grow all over Marin, San Francisco, and the Peninsula.

The harvest time varies with the sunniness of the location, but most plants appear between January and May. In irrigated lawns, you may find them at the harvesting stage anytime of year. As for myself, I am returning to a simple enjoyment of their cheery flowers and fetching seedheads.

Filaree or Storksbill *(Erodium cicutarium)*
Cranesbill or Wild Geranium *(Geranium molle)*

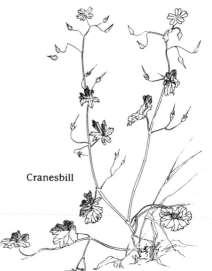

Cranesbill

These two European immigrants have settled on virtually all the open grasslands in the Bay Area. From February through June, their small, pink flowers enliven the green hillsides.

Wild geranium's leaves look exactly like miniatures of the lemon-scented geraniums cultivated in gardens. Both they and the filaree leaves are edible, raw or cooked. Since they do not become bitter, you can gather them anytime you see them. However, they are small, fuzzy, and tasteless, becoming waterlogged when cooked. Not one of the great wild edibles, but how much they contribute to each spring!

Broad-leaved Plantain *(Plantago major)*
Narrow-leaved Plantain *(P. lanceolata)*

The plantain pair are relatively attractive but tenacious lawn weeds. If they persist in spoiling your plans for a perfect lawn, you may find some comfort in regarding them as free food. Perhaps not especially tender or tasty food, but edible nonetheless.

Both plants grow in a rosette form, with the leaves coming out from a center at ground level. Broad-leaved plantain produces a low ring of rounded leaves on short stems, a little like large lollipops on short sticks. The narrow-leaved species has long, narrow leaves without stems and with veins that run the length of each leaf. Both species send up several flowering heads, each atop a slender stem. Once you learn to recognize these plants by name, you will probably realize that you have seen them often; both are widespread.

Broad-leaved Plantain

Broad-leaved plantain is the better tasting of the two species. If you gather its leaves when they are young, they make respectable cooked greens. The stems of the leaves are attached to the central stalk in the order of their development. I take the newest, still-unfolding leaf and the next-to-youngest one, whose stem attaches just below the new leaf. Usually, these plants grow in colonies, so one can afford to be so selective, but it may not be necessary. I find the leaves slightly too bitter even at that tender age, and mature leaves tend to have more bitterness than younger ones. However, if you enjoy the youngest plantain leaves, you may also like slightly older ones.

The stems are tougher than the leaves, so remove the stem ends. Simmering the leaves for five to ten minutes makes them very tender. If you like their flavor, then use them like any other greens. I didn't, so I sautéed the boiled greens in a little bacon fat, stirred in a dab of honey, and crumbled a piece of bacon over them. That completely masked their bitterness, and my husband loved the mixture. My sister didn't like honey and bacon flavors together, and refused to eat more than one bite. I liked them cooked that way, but what's the point of a food that that has to have sugar and saturated fat added to make it palatable?

Broad-leaved Plantain

After the plant flowers in the spring, it sets seeds. Some foraging books recommend drying the seeds and grinding them for use in pancakes or breads.

Where and When to Find It   The best places to find broad-leaved plantain are well-watered yards, golf courses, or park lawns. This species needs more water than is available in most natural settings here; however, scattered plants grow at the upper edges of the East Bay salt marshes. While this plantain is widespread, growing all over the Bay Area, it is not particularly common. You may need to look at a lot of lawns before you find it.

The best months to harvest the leaves tend to be late winter and spring. In a sunny location, March might be too late, whereas a shaded lawn can produce new leaves through May.

Narrow-leaved Plantain

This plantain ranks as a survival food rather than a vegetable one would choose freely. Even when very young, the leaves tend to be both bitter and tough, whereas the broad-leaved form at least is tender. I'm afraid I have nothing positive to say about its flavor.

If you wish to try it, you will have no trouble finding it. Common to abundant all over the Bay Area, it grows along roadsides, in lawns, on hills and in valleys, in grasslands, and in the packed earth of disturbed areas.

Where and When to Find It   Narrow-leaved plantain matures earlier than its broad-leaved cousin. In a year of heavy rains, it can be lush by October. Even in a normal year, the time to harvest it would be January or earlier.

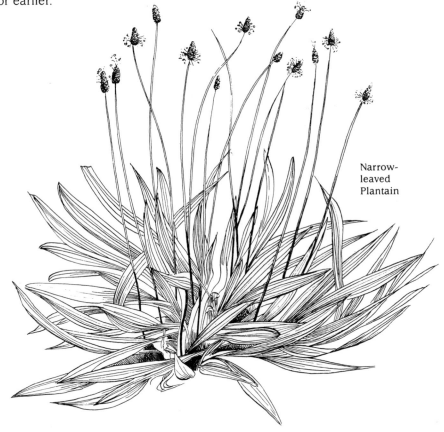

Narrow-
leaved
Plantain

Sow Thistle *(Sonchus oleraceus)*

Sow thistle has a lot going for it. It is easy to recognize because its yellow flowers look just like dandelion blossoms, but the plant commonly grows a foot tall or higher and the dark green, irregularly shaped leaves wrap around the stem in an unusual way. There is nothing prickly about them; the common name is absurd in that respect.

The plant could be a prototype for edible weeds. It came here from Europe, has become common in disturbed soil all over the Bay Area, and has tender, vitamin-rich leaves. As for taste, the leaves do tend to be bitter, even when young. Some people clearly like bitter flavors more than I do, or no one would eat dandelion greens; so if you are in that camp, you will probably become a fan of sow thistle. It is well worth trying, steamed or in a casserole, because everything else about the plant—availability, ease of recognition, tenderness—recommends it.

Sow Thistle

All the foraging guides say that one can reduce bitterness by plunging the leaves in boiling water for a minute, changing the water and repeating the process a time or two. That's never done the trick for me; if the leaves were too bitter to be enjoyable before the boiling, they have been so afterward as well. However, you might have better luck. I hope so.

Where and When to Find It   Sow thistle is common in yards and along paths and roadsides. You will find it throughout the Bay Area.

The leaves should be gathered before the plants bloom, which means you should gather them between December and May. In my neighbor's yard, they are ready for harvest in January and gone to seed by March. Four blocks away, in the deep shade of a forest, I find young plants in May. So harvesting time varies considerably within a small area, depending on the amount of sun a plant receives.

See also
Clover Leaves, page 198
Ice Plant, page 46
Nasturtium, page 33
Oxalis, page 31
Radish and Mustard Greens, page 26
Shepherd's Purse, page 207

CHAPTER 7

Mushrooms and Mushrooming

My grandmother tells of waking at 4 A.M. on summer mornings as a girl to go on mushrooming forays in rural Bohemia. She and her relatives knew where to find the most delicious species and returned from those dawn outings with a mouth-watering harvest. ✿ What a remote dream that always seemed to me! I grew up with a good case of fungophobia—an irrational fear of eating any wild mushrooms because of the few that are deadly. ✿ So it was with great pleasure that I discovered the Mycological Society of San Francisco. This salutary group offers anyone the opportunity to go on local mushroom hunts with a highly trained and experienced wild mushroom eater. The people on the walk bring the mushrooms they see to the leader, who explains how to identify them. Anyone lucky enough to find an edible one gets to take it home for lunch, secure in the knowledge of its safety.

I have not progressed very far yet. In the few times I have gone mushrooming, I have mostly found inedible ones—not poisonous, just bad tasting or indigestible. I have only been able to take one common species home. It was *Suillus pungens,* which has a slimy surface and spongy underside and is popular with maggots as it ages. For all its off-putting exterior, the peeled, inner flesh of the cap from a sound specimen tastes sweet and good, sautéed in a little butter. I was so thrilled to be finally tasting a wild mushroom that I thought it was terrific.

More experienced mushroomers on those same walks found a number of species that sounded delicious and were more physically attractive as well. Once you find an edible mushroom and learn to identify it, you can harvest more mushrooms from that spot indefinitely. This is because the mushroom you see above ground is not a plant in its own right. It is only the fruiting portion, like a berry, nut, or flower gone to seed. The main portion of the mushroom plant, corresponding to roots, stems, and leaves, is called the mycelium. It is an underground network of whitish threads, and it produces multiple mushrooms whenever conditions are right. Picking a mushroom does not hurt the mycelium any more than picking a berry hurts the bush. So each good mushroom spot you find has the potential to produce a fresh crop overnight, any time the weather is right.

Why bother, when you can buy mushrooms and know they are safe? In part because the only way to taste the almondy *Agaricus augustus* or the maple-syrup-scented candy cap is to learn to find them in the wild. The taste most of us associate with mushrooms is simply the flavor of the commercially grown *Agaricus bisporus* (or *Agaricus safewayensis,* as many mushroomers call it). Every other species has its own unique flavor, and most mushroom foragers plainly regard *A. bisporus* as a pale substitute for the savor waiting in the woods. Major Bay Area markets may now offer half a dozen mushroom varieties or more, but you still can't buy all the flavors you can find outdoors. And while a store-bought chanterelle may taste the same as a wild one, it can't provide the thrill of finding your own secret harvest site.

The limiting factor in the growth of mushrooms in this area is moisture. The air is always warm enough for them here, so the peak mushroom season corresponds exactly with the rainy months; they abound from November through March or April, depending on the year. In the off-season of May through October, mushrooms can still be found along irrigated lawns, parks, and golf courses, and under trees that catch and drip enough moisture from the coastal fog.

To whet your appetite, here is a sampling of the local species. The ones described here are considered easy to identify; when you have seen their key characteristics pointed out by a guide often enough to remember them, you can collect them on your own without undue worry. The information given here is not complete enough to use for identification purposes.

The Prince *(Agaricus augustus)*

Noted for its sweet, almondy taste when young, this becomes richly "mushroomy" when mature. It is good raw or cooked. The prince is not common, but since the caps grow up to 14 inches across, one alone provides a feast. It is a warm-weather mushroom, found from about February through October on north-facing, coastal, wooded slopes, particularly in the Presidio and in the redwood parks of the Peninsula.

Chanterelle *(Cantharellus cibarius)*

This much beloved mushroom can weigh up to a pound per specimen, and is cherished both for its golden color and its delicate, fruity aroma. For the best flavor, chanterelles should be simmered slowly for 1 to 1½ hours to remove their tannic acid. They grow away from the coast, appearing from late November through April or May. Typical habitats are on the eastern side of the Point Reyes ridges and in the Berkeley/ Hayward hills. Look for them in wet soil at the base of Douglas firs, tanbark oaks, and bay trees.

Chanterelles

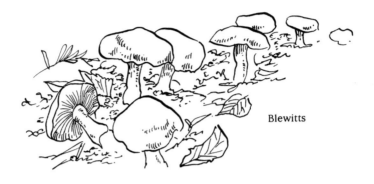

Blewitts

Blewitt *(Lepista nuda)*

These are abundant and full of flavor. They are also a lovely purple. Each mycelium produces many crops every season. Needing cold weather, they grow from December through February, under live oak, pine, and cypress trees. The Berkeley Marina is noted for a particularly good crop of them. Be sure to have an expert show you their identifying characteristics, since a poisonous purple mushroom also grows in the Bay Area.

Oyster Mushroom *(Pleurotus ostreatus)*

A classic winter mushroom, these are common after the big November rains and continue to appear through March. Their taste is said to be fishy and delicous; people press the moisture out of them with paper towels and then batter-fry them. Oyster mushrooms grow most commonly in canyons on tanoaks, live oaks, and bay trees; Redwood Regional Park in Oakland is a typical habitat.

~~~~~~

There are so many more, with names and flavors that sound delightful: puffballs, shaggy parasols, shaggy manes, candy caps, and the prized morels. Collecting them can be both enjoyable and safe, once you learn from an experienced mushroomer how to identify them.

Most of us are so afraid of wild mushrooms already that I hesitate to fan the flames of any more fear. But people do continue to die occasionally in the Bay Area from eating the wrong mushrooms. *This chapter should not be used as a guide for going out and nibbling some on your own.* The death cap, *Amanita phalloides,* has become quite common in parts of the Bay Area. Young ones are sometimes mistaken for the edible puffballs, and the mature ones can be seductively beautiful. The death angel also grows in our woods. Enough said? Wild mushrooms are to delight in, not to die for.

For More Information   For hands-on experience, the Mycological Society of San Francisco is the simplest way to go. This group also organizes field trips elsewhere in the Bay Area, so you may find them helpful even if you live far from San Francisco. You can contact them by writing to P.O. Box 11321, San Francisco 94101, or by calling (415) 759-0495.

To see several hundred labeled local species and to taste a mushroom dish or two, go to one of the society's Fungus Fairs. Each year they sponsor fairs in San Francisco in December and at Coyote Point Museum in San Mateo in January.

In addition to field trips, the society has monthly meetings, featuring movies, slides, or talks about topics of interest to mushroom hunters. They also have dinner meetings featuring mushroom recipes.

Morels, though uncommon here, can be found in localized abundance in the Sierras; the society sponsors outings to the mountains on spring weekends, from which most diligent searchers return well pleased.

The Academy of Sciences in San Francisco sponsors occasional mushroom-gathering field trips, typically to Mendocino or to the Academy's preserve near Santa Rosa, and other nature-exploration groups organize occasional local or north-coast outings. Santa Cruz has an active mushroom society, led by the highly respected (and witty) mushroom expert David Arora.

My two favorite books for Bay Area mushrooming are:

Mushrooms Demystified, by David Arora (Berkeley: Ten Speed Press, 1986). This is a thorough introduction to the identification, growing habits, and edibility of the mushrooms of the central California coast. It includes mushrooms from elsewhere in North America, but in less detail. The prose is unusually lighthearted and friendly for such an excellent and authoritative reference.

Mushrooms of San Francisco: A Walk on Land's End, by Roger Bland (San Francisco: Land's End Press, 1978). This is a slim volume devoted to the mushrooms of Lincoln Park. It is useful as reinforcement for what you can learn on the Mycological Society's walks there, and includes a map showing which edible species grow where. Just remember that however much you may teach yourself using this or other guides, beginners should show the mushrooms they collect to someone who is experienced before eating them. The book seems to be out of print, so you may have to do some digging to obtain a copy.

Additionally, some experienced mushroomers recommend *Mushrooms and Other Common Fungi of the San Francisco Bay Region,* by Robert and Dorothy Orr (Berkeley: University of California Press, 1962) and *The Mushrooms of Northern California* by David Biek (Redding: Spore Print, 1984).

CHAPTER 8

Seaweeds and Their Seasons

O f all the things I learned while doing the research for this book, the strangest was that seaweeds are edible and can be gathered and cooked like any other wild vegetables. They look so alien from land plants. Chewing them at the beach does nothing to alter that impression; most raw seaweeds taste like rubber or plastic. But some species have become welcome items in my diet. Though it still feels odd to react this way to a seaweed, finding a harvest-sized blade of one of my favorites can make me salivate. ✿ Usually the best low tides are fairly early in the morning, and while it is hard to get out of bed so quickly on a weekend, once at the shore, I'm charmed by the sparkly gold-toned light, the solitude, and the fresh saltiness of the air. It feels good to wake up that way for a change. I like balancing on the wet rocks in my oldest sneakers, feeling an occasional, cold wavelet or puddle shock my feet, and snooping around examining blades like a fussy shorebird.

Why Eat Seaweeds?   The best seaweed species absorb the flavors with which they are cooked, concentrating the essence of a sauce or soup into flavorful bites. Contrary to expectations, seaweeds are not salty. They develop a satisfying chewiness as they cook, much like pasta al dente, calamari, or certain mushrooms. I value them for the texture and excitement they contribute to a meal. Even cooked, seaweeds harbor traces of the exotic and romantic associations we attach to seashores.

Many species are traditional foods in the coastal communities of Northern Europe, Asia, and Hawaii, providing essential vitamins and minerals free for the gathering. In the food-rich Bay Area, there is little incentive to harvest seaweeds for their nutritional value. However, learning to recognize several species and tasting them will offer you other, more unusual benefits. To eat something is to know it in only the most primitive sense, but often prompts the observations that lead to a more intimate under-

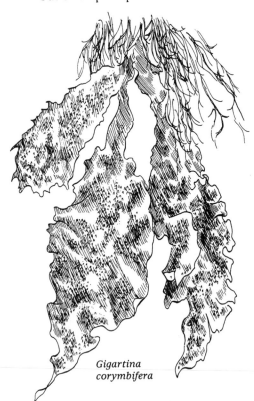

Gigartina corymbifera

standing. Bending down to sort through species for the most appetizing blades, I have begun to notice patterns of growth and reproductive structures that I would never have seen if the seaweeds had remained an undifferentiated jumble in my mind. We pay closest attention to those things which are of concrete value to us.

Ocean plants, like land plants, require particular habitats. Some species thrive under the battering waves of an exposed, rocky coast. Others are adapted to the gentle waters of a bay or the brackish water where a stream enters the ocean. Furthermore, seaweeds are divided into sun-loving and shade-tolerating species, just like land plants. Shade on the ocean floor increases as the water becomes deeper or more cloudy, because sunlight is filtered out by the particles suspended in the water. All seaweeds need some sunlight since it supplies the energy for their growth, so where the water is so deep that no light reaches the bottom, no plants grow. Each species grows best at a particular depth, depending on how much light it needs.

Foragers care most about the species that need so much light they are uncovered by the low tide. Any species that grows where it is underwater during high tide but is exposed during low tide is *intertidal.* Plants in this group must adapt to the temperature extremes and drying effects of air and to being pounded by water when the tide moves over them. Fortunately for us, some of the best edible ones are uncovered often; others, needing less sun, are uncovered only during the lowest tides of the year.

A species that can survive in the dimly lit subtidal region, where no low tide ever uncovers it, is protected from the drastic extremes of alternating water and air environments. Subtidal species are seen only when a storm tears them loose from their normally placid moorings and casts them up on the beach, or when they die and float in to shore.

A coastal forager also learns that seaweeds are as seasonal in their growth patterns as land plants. A beach can be relatively clean and bare in January and lush with seaweeds by April. Seaweeds grow in response to the increased sunshine filtering down to them in spring and summer, and die back when the days grow short in late autumn. A drought year will speed up their growth somewhat because of all the extra sun. But in general, since the same amount of water is available to them the year round, drought or wet years don't affect them greatly, so their growing seasons do not vary much from year to year.

Who ever thinks of spring coming to the shoreline? Yet, once you are familiar with the summer appearance of mature seaweeds, it can be a very sweet experience to go to a beach at low tide in March and see all the same species, still tiny but perfectly formed.

Seaweed Foraging in the Bay Area   The Bay Area may have the best coast for edible seaweeds in the world. We take second place for number of species, after Australia and New Zealand, and we tie with Japan for sheer quantity. Of the shorelines that botanists have studied, the west coast of the United States is unparalleled in its combination of variety and abundance.

Conservation The abundance we enjoy is not infinite. In 1984, it became illegal to collect one edible species, the sea palm, because the plants were under too much harvesting pressure. Sea palms are wonderful to look at, swaying on wave-beaten rocks like trees in a tropical storm, creating perfect miniature islands on any rock they colonize. I hope they return to their former numbers.

I have heard reports of northern beaches being illegally swept clean of edible species. The casual forager is not to blame for this; rangers patrol for people filling up pickup trucks. But as seaweeds become more popular, even modest foraging can take a cumulative toll. To soften our impact and prolong the period when harvesting seaweeds for personal use is relatively easy, please be realistic about quantities. Especially in the beginning, just take a blade or two home to try in one dish. If you take more, the chances are high that you will let it sit in the refrigerator until it rots. Then, on its way to the garbage can, it will mock you for having torn it from its native habitat. I speak from experience. Keep your harvests modest, cherish the resource, and keep ecoguilt at bay.

The legal limit for collection keeps dropping. Currently, at most state beaches, the limit is ten pounds, net weight. At special ecological reserves no collecting is allowed. Point Reyes has been following the state limit but could always change, and portions of the GGNRA have lower limits, so (as usual) you need to ask before you pick.

Safety A big plus for local seaweed eaters is the absence of dangerous species. You can chew on any seaweed you find without fear of serious consequences. There is one group, the *Desmarestia* species, that contains sulfuric acid in sufficient concentration to make some people

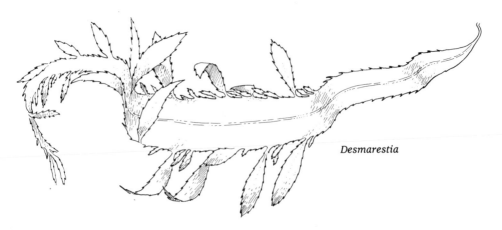

Desmarestia

nauseous. However, other people, apparently less sensitive, use these species in soups for their sour, acid flavor.

The *Desmarestias* do not look like any of the other seaweeds eaten locally. In the unlikely event that you do bring some home by mistake, you will be warned by their tendency to bleach the color from and turn to mush the other species in your collecting bag. (The acid dissolves them just as acids in our stomachs dissolve our food.) *Desmarestia* grows in several forms here, typically brown or tan colored, but sometimes olive green. It usually has a conspicuous vein running up the center of the plant and a ragged look due to the many tiny bladelets along its edges.

Terminology   Seaweed structures are described in different terms than land plants, with the words *blade, stipe,* and *holdfast.* Most seaweeds are attached to rocks, pilings, or other objects. The part of the plant that grips the rocks is called the holdfast. The leafy portion of the plant is called the blade. Some seaweeds have a thin, tough stem or a long, hollow one connecting the holdfast to the blade, and that stem is known as the stipe.

Tides   You need to know when the tide will be low enough to uncover the seaweeds. Newspapers publish the time and height of each day's tides, but in order to plan ahead, you'll need to get a tide table. These booklets show a whole year's tides and are sold or given away in sporting goods and fishing supply stores.

We have two low tides each day, one significantly lower than the other. The lowest tides, which do not happen every day or even every week, drop below the low tide line (or mark). Such tides are called *minus tides* and are shown on tide tables as negative numbers (feet below the low-tide line). A number of seaweeds are only visible during minus tides, and the lower the minus tide, the more you'll see. At least a few weekends each spring and summer have excellent minus tides during daylight hours.

Note that the times given in local tide tables are accurate for the Golden Gate. If you want to catch low tide at any beach other than Ft. Point (which lies in the shadow of the Golden Gate Bridge), use the chart at the back of the tide table to adjust the time for your location. For example, low tide occurs at Point Reyes 1 hour and 12 minutes earlier than it does at the Golden Gate.

Preparation   Your seaweeds will taste best if you follow some simple rules in handling them. Like any green vegetables, fresh seaweeds deteriorate at room temperature and are preserved by cold. Unless you are going to use them right away, refrigerate your seaweeds in a plastic bag or airtight container. Do not wash them first, since salt water helps to preserve them. Most will stay fresh for close to a week if refrigerated promptly.

Many species can be dried for later use. Unless they are free of sand, wash them before drying. Use lukewarm water, since cold water will not loosen all the grit and hot water may release the gels in the blades, making them gooey. Rinse the plants as quickly as possible to protect their nutrients and flavors.

If the day is breezy and sunny, you can lay the plants on the grass, a towel, or a clothesline outdoors. Turn them once or twice to dry them thoroughly. Alternately, you can dry them in the oven. Lay the plants on a cookie sheet and bake them at 200° F. for about 30 minutes, turning them once. Leave the oven door open a crack so that moisture can escape.

Seaweeds dried too slowly begin to ferment and develop a strong odor and taste. Unless you like that quality (and some seaweed lovers do), avoid drying them outdoors on overcast or cool days or indoors in any weather.

Dried seaweeds should not be refrigerated. Store them in airtight bags or containers away from dampness or bright light. You can add them directly to soups or other dishes containing adequate moisture. For other uses, rehydrate the plants by briefly soaking them in water.

For More Information   The Ft. Point Ranger Station in San Francisco is a good place to begin. The most varied collection of seaweeds in the Bay Area grows directly in front of the station. You need a ranger's permission to collect seaweeds there, but it is an ideal place to learn to identify them.

Naturally, this being the Bay Area, occasional field trips and workshops are offered on edible seaweeds. Alice Green, who was my teacher, periodically offers spring workshops that include identification in the field and preparation and tasting of numerous seaweed dishes. She can be contacted at (415) 731-2506. The Point Reyes Field Seminars program also offers spring or summer workshops some years; call (415) 663-1200.

To pursue the subject further, you may find the following books interesting. For identifying seaweeds, there are two outstanding reference books with extraordinary illustrations, but each is a hefty and expensive tome of the sort you might want to borrow from a library rather than buy: *Marine Algae of California,* by I. A. Abbot and G. J. Hollenberg (Stanford: Stanford University Press, 1976) and *Marine Algae of the Monterey Peninsula,* by G. M. Smith (Stanford: Stanford University Press, 1969). Both contain scientific illustrations so detailed and lifelike that a layperson can identify many fresh specimens just by flipping through the pictures. To identify local species that are not included in this chapter, these are the books to turn to.

For more recipes and tidbits of seaweed lore, try *Sea Vegetables: Harvesting Guide and Cookbook* by Evelyn McConnaughey (Happy Camp: Naturegraph, 1985) or *Vegetables from the Sea to Help You Look and Feel Better* by Seibin and Teruko Arasaki (Tokyo: Japan Publications, 1983).

Two books I like are currently out of print. Here's a description of them anyway, because you may be able to find them through a secondhand bookstore: *The Sea Vegetable Book,* by Judith Cooper Madlener (New York: Clarkson N. Potter, 1977), discusses edible seaweeds from all over the world and includes over 100 recipes for them. *Common Seaweeds of the Pacific Coast,* by J. Robert Waaland (Seattle: Pacific Search Press, 1977), is an excellent introduction to the biology of seaweeds, with scientific descriptions and photographs of many common species. This is a paperback you can take to the seashore, thus filling a gap between foraging books and library tomes.

Alaria *(Alaria marginata)*

Alaria is easy to recognize. It has long, olive green or amber brown blades with gently ruffled edges and a firm midrib running the length of each blade. The blades reach maturity in midsummer, by which time they range from several to 12 feet long. The blades are attached to the rocks by a small holdfast and a thin, tough stipe.

The blade, including the midrib, makes a delicious addition to soups or vegetable dishes. Alaria's own flavor is unobtrusive, and it contributes a texture similar to some Chinese mushrooms. As it cooks, it turns an attractive green color.

Alaria is best when used fresh; drying can alter its flavor. I like to slice it into bite-sized pieces and saute it with other vegetables, such as

Alaria

peppers, mushrooms, spinach, onions, or broccoli, seasoning the blend with chopped ginger root and garlic. Even though one might expect them to be full of moisture, edible seaweeds are prone to drying out, so add a splash of water or sherry to the stir-fry, if needed.

From late June through September, I have found large clumps of alaria cast up on the beach near Ft. Point. When you can get alaria in drift form and it still smells fresh, that's the most ecologically sound way to harvest it.

If you are going to harvest a living plant, then take only the half of the blade furthest from the holdfast. That leaves the growing and reproductive portion intact, down near the juncture with the stipe. It also leaves enough blade area to photosynthesize sunlight and provide energy to the growing portion. Since alaria is not common here, it is especially important to protect the plants you find. Half of a mature blade, when it is several feet long, will often be even more than you want.

Where and When to Find It   Alaria grows on exposed rocks at or below the low-tide mark, so look for it during a very low tide. It grows at Ft. Point, at Ft. Cronkhite, and at Point Reyes near the end of Pierce Point Road.

In March, the blades are only 2 to 8 inches long, perfect miniatures of their mature forms. By late April, they are usually close to 2 feet long, but still a good deal smaller than their mature length. This is one of the few seaweeds that is truly at its best from mid-summer through mid-fall; look for it from late June through October. By December, the surviving blades are tattered and storm-tossed, soon to be replaced by next year's infant plants.

Sister Sarah *(Cystoseira osmundacea)*

This seaweed gets its common name from its Latin one; try saying *Cystoseira* aloud. It grows subtidally, underwater even during the lowest tides, so we only see it as drift. The air bladders are the most distinctive portion of the plant. They form little chains or stacks of balls, each one slightly smaller than the one below it, until the last one ends in a point.

Most fresh seaweeds have no particular flavor, but those air-bladder chains taste distinctly like raw peas. They have a similar mix of sweetness and mild bitterness. Their taste and texture even when raw are pleasant enough that I have actually swallowed some of the *Cystoseira* that I've nibbled at the beach. That's not true of any other seaweed species.

Sister
Sarah

Sister Sarah can grow up to 20 feet long, so you may find it in a large, tangled heap on the beach. More commonly, you will see just a piece with several air-bladder chains on it. The air bladders are the edible part. They turn a brighter green when cooked, and are good in tempura or in stir-fries, as long as they are surrounded by enough steam during cooking.

Where and When to Find It

Since *Cystoseira* comes up in drifts, you may find it on a beach far from where it grows. It is a species of the open coast rather than the Bay. I've seen it at Pigeon Point, Stinson Beach, and Palomarin.

May seems to be a good month to look for it. I've found large clumps then that passed the freshness test: Does the plant smell fresh? Do the bladders snap crisply or are they old enough to be softening? Because it is drift, you always need to check for freshness.

Green Nori *(Enteromorpha intestinalis)*

Green nori is primarily used to make a fragrant, nutty powder that is sprinkled over other foods. The plant is made of numerous long, thin, unbranched strands colored a clear, deep green. They lie flat like brushed hair on the sand or mudflats. The strands range in length from ½ inch up to a foot, but are only about ¼ inch wide.

One local species of sea lettuce looks similar but does not have as pleasant an aroma, so it is worth distinguishing between the two. Sea lettuce has a flat blade, whereas this nori has a flattened, hollow tube. You can slide the tube's walls around between your finger and thumb or break a strand in half and see the structure that way. Both species have the twisted, shiny look of the cellophane grass used in children's Easter baskets.

To try green nori, first clean it thoroughly. Bring home a fistful or two, immerse it in a pot of water, and swish it around. Usually some tiny snails and pebbles will fall to the bottom. Repeat once or twice with fresh water until no more grit separates out.

Either dry your nori in the sun or put it in a pie plate in a 150 to 200° F. oven for about 20 minutes until it crumbles when touched. One recipe called for toasting it afterward by holding the dry mass over a flame. I held some about 4 inches over the flame on our gas range and it instantly caught fire, so if you want to toast yours, hold it considerably higher or use a very low flame.

Crumble the dried nori into a powder with your fingers and put it in an empty salt shaker or spice container to sprinkle over soups, salads, or vegetable and rice dishes. Its mild flavor is pleasant and it contains a number of useful minerals.

Where and When to Find It   This seaweed does best in calm waters of reduced salinity, so look for it wherever a stream or rainwater drainage

Green Nori

pipe enters the ocean or the Bay. It grows at the St. Francis Yacht Harbor in San Francisco, at Ft. Point, in Bolinas Lagoon, and at Palomarin Beach. I'm not sure how clean the water is at the Yacht Harbor.

Peak harvest time is in early to mid-spring, so April would be an ideal month to forage for it. Green nori grows near the high-tide mark, so any low tide will uncover it.

Bladderwrack or Rockweed *(Fucus vesiculosis)*

This is one of the most common seaweeds on the exposed rocks of the open coast. Its color ranges from olive green to brown, and it is notable for the bean-sized air bladders built into the blades. If you went to any rocky beach as a child, you probably spent time popping those air sacs between your fingers.

The blades are narrow and branching, with a vein running up the center. The plants average a foot long or less. Since the blades are relatively thick and tough, they are not usually eaten.

Instead, bladderwrack is used as a flavoring agent. Washed, chopped coarsely, and dried, it can be steeped as a pleasant tea. Fresh, it is the traditional seaweed of choice for clambakes. The clams are steamed between layers of moist rockweed, so that the sweet aroma of the plant is transferred to the shellfish.

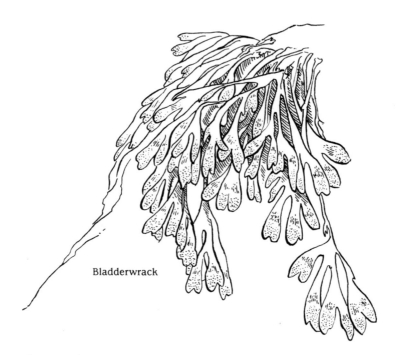

Bladderwrack

If you make a clam chowder or other seafood soup, try adding a large handful of washed rockweed to a quart of broth. Simmer the rockweed for 10 minutes and then strain it out of the broth before adding the other soup ingredients. It will darken the liquid and transfer to it a fragrance both sweet and reminiscent of clams.

Where and When to Find It   Rockweed is abundant along Bay Area shores. You'll find it at Pigeon Point, Bean Hollow Beach, Pillar Point, Ft. Cronkhite, Palomarin, and numerous other beaches. It is also thick along the sea wall bordering the Marina Green in San Francisco. You might want to learn to identify it there and do your collecting in more assuredly clean waters.

This seaweed is especially full of vitamins and minerals, some of which will transfer to the tea or broth you make. The plants have their highest Vitamin A content in summer and their highest Vitamin C content in early fall. By November, many blades look scruffy and worn, and the next year's plants are quite small until about April. Rockweed grows near the low-tide mark.

Turkish Bath Towel *(Gigartina exasperata)*
Grapestone *(Petrocelis middendorffii,* formerly *Gigartina papillata)*

These two are fun to use. Their dark, brownish red blades are covered with thousands of small bumps. When you chop the blades for cooking, the bumps make the pieces jump around on the cutting board. The bumps are rounded on some blades and pointed on others. On the large blades of the bath-towel species, the bumps occasionally grow tiny, branched projections of their own. The look and feel of the blades is reminiscent of rough terry cloth, hence the common name.

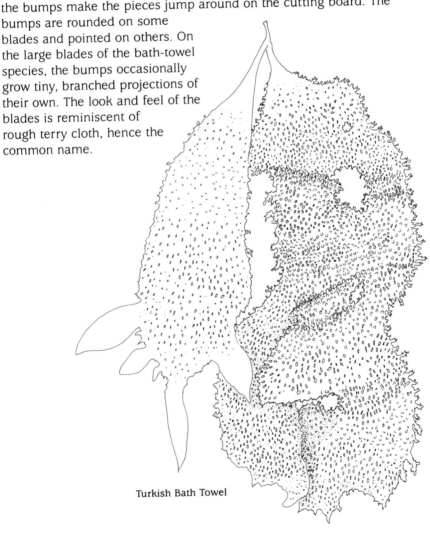

Turkish Bath Towel

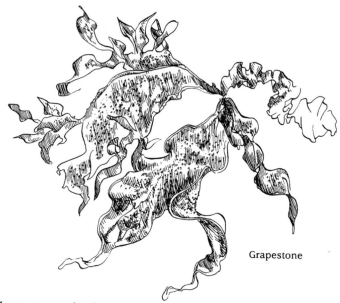

Grapestone

Many seaweeds alternate between sexual and asexual generations. Both generations produce spores, but the spores from asexual plants can germinate and grow on their own, whereas for the sexual generations, reproductive matter from both male and female blades must meet and fuse to produce viable spores. The *Gigartina papillata* name is being changed to *Petrocelis middendorffii* because botanists have decided that it represents the sexual phases in the life cycle of *P. middendorffii,* previously thought to be strictly asexual.

The little grapestone species grows on rocks relatively high in the intertidal zone, and stands 3 to 6 inches tall. You will have no trouble finding it, as it is one of the most common seaweeds on this coast. The Turkish bath towel is less common intertidally, but very noticeable wherever it grows. Mature blades are a foot or longer and as broad as your outstretched fingers.

Both species contain almost 50 percent carrageenan by dry weight. This thickener is extracted and used commercially: you will see it as an ingredient in many prepared foods when a smooth, jelled quality is desired.

At home, you can use these seaweeds as a substitute for gelatin when making vegetable aspics. Since gelatin is an animal product, *Gigartina* offers vegetarians a way to have their principles and aspic, too.

Most books on edible seaweeds also contain recipes for dessert puddings thickened with seaweed, but I don't recommend the concoctions.

I tried a peanut-butter pudding and a pineapple blanc mange, and in each instance, a seaweed aftertaste was noticeable. The same flavor that adds intrigue to an aspic can spell disaster for a dessert.

If you do make a sweet pudding, my advice is to eat it quickly. When my husband wolfed some down, he thought it tasted fine, but when he was less hungry and let the flavor linger in his mouth, he didn't like it. The seaweed flavor seems to register toward the rear of the tongue, whereas sweetness registers nearer the front. If you eat something in a hurry, the food goes from the front of your mouth to your throat with hardly a pause along the way.

Where and When to Find Them   It is hard to think of a rocky shoreline in the Bay Area where grapestone *doesn't* grow. You will find it at Pigeon Point, Bean Hollow Beach, Ft. Point, and abundantly at Palomarin. The Turkish bath towel is less common, but does appear in most of those places. Grapestone will be uncovered by the lowest tide most days, whereas you'll need a minus tide to see Turkish bath towel.

Unless the winter is unusually long and rainy, these seaweeds are large enough to harvest by April. They continue to be in season through the fall, though by November much of the grapestone is worn thin and frayed at the tips.

VEGETARIAN TOMATO ASPIC

- 1 cup Turkish bath towel or grapestone
- 4 cups tomato or V-8 juice
- ½ lemon
- 1 tablespoon sherry
- Worcestershire sauce

Thoroughly wash the seaweed in lukewarm water and chop it coarsely. Add the seaweed to the V-8 juice or tomato juice. Simmer gently 25 minutes, stirring occasionally. This will distribute the carrageenan as the heat draws it from the seaweed.

Then add the lemon juice and Worcestershire sauce to taste. Simmer 5 more minutes. Pour the mixture through a strainer to remove the plants. Chill the aspic until cold and jelled. Garnish with thin lemon slices.

Ogo *(Gracilaria verrucosa)*

Ogo lies like brown spaghetti on the sand. The strands are round, thin, and about a foot long. Each strand branches a few times, but the overall effect is straight rather than bushy.

Seaweed lovers enjoy mixing blanched ogo with spaghetti. With a sauce made from tomatoes, fish, and herbs, the maritime flavors enhance each other and the dish works well.

Ogo is also quite good with a highly seasoned dressing. The recipe is Alice Green's variation on ogo kim chee, the traditional Korean ogo pickle.

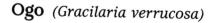

Ogo

ALICE GREEN'S OGO KIM CHEE

- 2 cups ogo
- 1½ teaspoons salt
- ¼ cup chopped green onions
- ¼ teaspoon cayenne pepper
- 1 tablespoon minced garlic
- 2 tablespoons toasted sesame seeds
- ½ teaspoon grated ginger root
- ¼ cup each vinegar and soy sauce

Pour boiling water over the ogo in a bowl. Add salt and let it sit for half an hour. Drain. Chop into 4-inch lengths. Add remaining ingredients and serve.

Where and When to Find It   Ogo grows on sand, mudflats, or rocks from the midtidal zone downward. It grows most abundantly in sheltered waters, but can be found along the open coast. So, while you can find it at Pigeon Point and Bean Hollow, for example, it is more common at Ft. Point and is abundant at Bolinas Lagoon.

Unusual weather patterns can alter the normal distribution of sea-weeds. The winters of '81–'82 and '82–'83 were much longer and wetter than normal. In 1983, little ogo appeared in Bolinas Lagoon, presumably because the heavy runoff had made the lagoon too fresh (unsalty) to support the species that year.

Ogo contains a gelling agent called agar. Its agar content is highest in spring, so ogo is collected then to extract the gel. However, as a food, ogo is at its best in summer. May, June, and July yield better harvests than August. By late summer, the sunlight bleaches much of the ogo a pale tan, making it less appetizing.

Ogo

Iridaea *(Iridaea cordata)*

This species is worth learning to recognize, if only because it is so beautiful. Until it was pointed out to me, I had never noticed it, but now I seek it out, just to admire its colors.

From some angles, iridaea is a smooth, hand-sized sheet of dull, purplish brown—definitely on the dreary side. But when the sun shines on a wet blade, the plant is transformed. Lying in shallow pools, it glows a midnight blue-purple, highlighted with irridescent colors like those in a drop of oil.

Iridaea can be used as a thickening agent in exactly the same way as grapestone. It, too, is 50 percent carrageenan by dry weight. But since grapestone is so abundant and iridaea so lovely, the latter is best left as a feast for the eyes.

Where and When to Find It   I have seen it at Ft. Point, Pigeon Point, and Palomarin. It grows in the lower intertidal area, so look for it on a minus tide.

The blades appear as early as March, but they are small then, and their irridescence is not as evident as it will become later. By May, the species is more striking, and it continues to be beautiful through the summer and early fall.

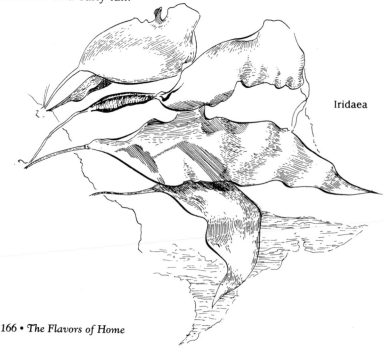

Iridaea

Laminaria or Kombu *(Laminaria sinclairii)*

Laminaria grows in bunches on rocks. The brown blades are up to a yard or more in length but only an inch or 2 wide. They are flat and smooth. Each blade is attached to the rocks by a thin, very tough, black stipe. Laminaria has one of the simplest shapes and is one of the easiest seaweeds to recognize in the Bay Area.

The local laminaria is too tough to eat, but the blades give a refined Japanese flavor to soup stocks. Try adding 8 to 12 inches of blade to 3 cups of water or chicken stock. Simmer gently for a few minutes. Then remove the seaweed and add whatever other seasonings or ingredients you like.

When harvesting a blade, cut it off at least 3 inches above the stipe. The growing portion of the blade is in the first 3 inches and it will regenerate itself if that part is intact.

Where and When to Find It   Laminaria grows lushly at Ft. Point, Pillar Point, and McClure's Beach at Point Reyes. Look for it during a minus tide, since it grows low in the intertidal zone.

Spring and summer are considered the best seasons to harvest it, but it can be found through December.

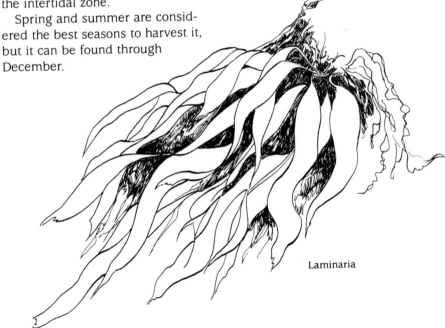

Laminaria

Bull Whip Kelp

Bull Whip Kelp *(Nereocystis luetkeana)*

Bull whip kelp generally grows in beds far deeper than any tide lays bare, but individual specimens are occasionally tossed onto our beaches by the waves. The stipes are hollow tubes up to 120 feet long, each ending in a round, hollow bulb. The air trapped in the bulb and stipe pulls the kelp up so that the blades float close to the surface and receive adequate sunlight. The numerous blades are like long, slender petals, sprouting from the top of the bulb.

There are two main uses for this unlikely looking food. The blades are not usually eaten, but the bulb and stem sections can be made into pickles, just as we pickle cucumbers or watermelon rind or any other firm vegetable. The stems can also be used to make cake in the same way that carrots are used. Though this sounds bizarre, it tastes quite normal.

For eating, kelp should be young—not more than 15 feet long or 3 inches in diameter. And it must be fresh. Bend the stem at one of the ends. If it bends like soft rubber, it is old. You want the ones that snap crisply in two.

To make kelp cake, cut a stem into strips so that you can pack it into a quart jar. You will need one jar of stems for each layer of cake. Fill the jar with fresh water and refrigerate it. Change the water once a day for four days. Then grate the stem and substitute the grated kelp for the carrot in your favorite carrot cake recipe. One packed jar yields about 1½ cups of grated kelp.

To be honest, making a cake with kelp was emotionally difficult the first time. The whole idea seemed so alien that I waited two weeks rather than four days, by which time the refrigerated kelp was becoming decidedly limp. The fact that it still worked well is a testament to the keeping quality of the plant. Then, when I did grate the stuff, a powerful aroma of iodine rose up. It seemed wasteful to adulterate the other ingredients with such a substance, but a ranger I trust had promised me that kelp cake was delicious, so I proceeded strictly on faith.

During the baking, the iodine aroma disappeared. The pieces of kelp look like citron, so they were easy to accept visually. And, like zucchini, the more orthodox carrot substitute, the kelp contributed moisture without adding any detectable flavor of its own. We had a party that night, and the kelp cake was a definite success.

I am still loyal to carrots; they contain more Vitamin A than kelp and they are easier to use. But I like seeing bull whip kelp on the beach now, knowing that I could eat it and enjoy it if I wanted to.

Where and When to Find It   Since kelp comes ashore as drift, it can turn up on almost any beach, far from the nearest kelp bed. It washes up between Baker Beach and Ft. Point, for example, and certainly you will see it on the beaches of the outer coast.

While the big storms of winter do cast up massive specimens, they are generally too large or old for eating. The best time to forage for bull whip kelp is in August and September when smaller plants frequently wash ashore.

Nori *(Porphyra lanceolata)*
Laver or Nori *(P. perforata)*

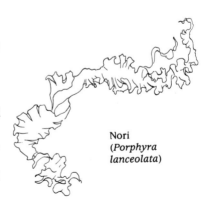

Nori
(*Porphyra
lanceolata*)

Neither of these seaweeds is really nori. That's the Japanese name for the most favored seaweed that grows in Japanese waters; the same species does not occur here. However, these two *Porphyras* make good substitutes for the real thing. People who eat the local seaweeds tend to call them both nori and gloss over the distinctions between them.

Both local species produce sheer, glossy, ruffled blades that attach directly to the rocks with no visible stipe. Their color ranges from a steel grey to grey-green to brownish purple. *Porphyra lanceolata's* blades are long and thin (lancelike), whereas *P. perforata's* blades are often as broad as they are long. At the beginning of a low tide, the *Porphyras* are more obvious, glistening in tousled heaps on the shallowest rocks. Later, as the sun dries them, they flatten, and only their color and location hint at the identity of the glossy, dark streaks plastered to the rocks.

The blades of either species are delicately chewy when steamed or simmered for 5 minutes. They are delicious in stir-fries, but only if you protect them from drying out by adding a bit of liquid. Try wrapping nori around pieces of fish, dipping them in a batter, and sautéeing them. The seaweed keeps the fish moist.

Nori is wonderful in soups, and adds particular flair to delicate, clear ones like egg flower soup. If you bake the blades for 30 minutes at 200° F. with the oven door slightly ajar, the dried nori will keep almost indefinitely in a plastic bag or airtight container. It's easy to rehydrate it by soaking the pieces briefly in water, and then you can add nori to meals whenever you wish.

Where and When to Find Them   The *Porphyras* are common at Ft. Point, Ft. Cronkhite, Palomarin, and elsewhere. They grow relatively high in the intertidal zone, so any minus tide will uncover them.

The peak harvest is from May through August; before that, the plants are too small, and by autumn, many of them are bleached from sunlight.

Nori
(*Porphyra
lanceolata*)

Sea Lettuce *(Ulva lactuca)*

This is a cheery, bright green seaweed that really does look a bit like a lettuce leaf. The name is misleading, though, in encouraging people to eat the blades raw. They are okay in salads but definitely on the tough, plastic side. I had a low opinion of sea lettuce until I cooked it. Then it became tender. In fact, partly because of the other, wonderful ingredients, it was a part of the most successful seaweed recipe I've tried.

Sea lettuce is at its best in the spring, coinciding with asparagus season. I sautéed some asparagus very briefly in butter, then added the sea lettuce. Like most seaweeds, it becomes most tender if it is cooked in liquid, as opposed to being sautéed. In a damn-the-cholesterol mood, I simmered the vegetables in a little cream flavored with splashes of sherry and soy sauce. Sea lettuce should only be cooked for about 10 minutes, like so many leafy greens. When there were only a few minutes left in the cooking time, I added some shrimp, just to heat them through, and the result was splendid. The sea lettuce became delicious because it soaked up the other flavors, and it contributed a pretty color and pleasantly chewy texture of its own.

You can also use this species in the same ways you would use alaria or nori: in soups, sautéed with moist vegetables, particularly mushrooms, or wrapped around fish pieces and fried. Some people like it raw in salads. If you use it raw, chop it into bite-sized pieces. When cooking sea lettuce in liquid, it is better to leave the blades intact or to tear them only once or twice. Otherwise, if the pieces are both tender and tiny, they will seem to disappear in your mouth; the flavor is so delicate that you will have a hard time tasting it amidst the other ingredients.

The pedant in me feels obliged to point out that most of the time you think you are eating the official sea lettuce, *Ulva lactuca,* you will actually be eating *Ulva expansa* or *U. lobata.* Both are far more common on this coast, grow in the same places, and can only be distinguished from *U. lactuca* with a microscope. As far as I can tell, it makes absolutely no difference which ones we eat.

Where and When to Find It   Sea lettuce thrives in brackish water, where a stream or other fresh-water source enters the ocean and dilutes the salinity of the water. For example, it grows at Ft. Point because a pipe there drains a spring from the neighboring hillside. It grows on the Palomarin coast of Point Reyes where a stream flows into the ocean. In rainy years, with heavy fresh-water flows, there's noticeably more of it than in dry years.

Sea Lettuce

   This species also thrives on organic pollution, so when you find a sea lettuce patch, think about where the nearest fresh water is coming from. Use caution if the water might be contaminated by cows upstream or by septic-tank drainage. By the way, even though Ft. Point is in the Bay, its water is relatively clean because the tides bring new ocean water in along the edges of the Bay, whereas the outgoing, dirtier water leaves through the center of the Golden Gate, far from the shoreline seaweeds. The farther you are from the Golden Gate, the less vigorous the Bay's tidal flushing becomes and the more conservative you might want to be about eating seaweeds.

   Sea lettuce is an early-growing species. By March, it is already well developed; not quite full sized, but much farther along than most other seaweeds. It is most tender then, although in late spring it has a higher Vitamin C content. The plants thrive at least through September. By November they become scarce.

   Sea lettuce grows at the lower end of the intertidal zone. You will need a minus tide to see much of it.

OTHER EDIBLE SEAWEEDS THAT GROW IN THE BAY AREA

I've included the following species for the sake of completeness, but can't write about them with the enthusiasm I feel for the others. Nibbles and sea fir I haven't found yet, though I know they are here. Sea sac, sea petals, and stone hair are not too difficult to find, but just haven't captured my imagination as foodstuffs.

Each of us can have such different experiences with the same raw materials that some of these may end up being your favorites.

Nibbles *(Ahnfeltia gigartinoides)*

This plant has thin, stiff, many-branched strands colored deep red to purplish black, about 4 to 12 inches long. It is found on intertidal or subtidal rocks south of Pacifica and at Pillar Point. Harvest it from early spring to early fall. Chopped finely, it can be added to meat dishes for flavor and thickening.

Sea Fir or Fir Needles *(Analipus japonicus)*

Its greenish brown fronds grow up to 14 inches tall. Each frond looks like a twig from a fir tree, with "needles" growing out in all directions from the stem. The base is perennial, but the fronds grow up new each year. Found on rocks at Palomarin Beach in Point Reyes, sea fir is harvested from May through October. Fresh plants are used in soups.

Sea Petals or Flower Seaweed *(Petalonia fascia)*

The flat blades of this plant grow up to 14 inches long, tapering to a point where they attach to rocks. They grow in clusters and are olive brown to dark brown in color. Positive identification may be impossible without a microscope, but the species that it resembles can be used the same ways. Sea petals grows on upper to midtidal rocks at Ft. Point and along the Point Reyes coast near Arch Rock. It can be harvested from spring through fall. The plant can be used as a substitute for wakame, a popular Japanese seaweed that does not grow in California. Add the blades to soups or stir-fries.

Sea Sac *(Halosaccion glandiforme)*

This seaweed consists of clusters of sacs, usually 2 to 6 inches tall, attached to a holdfast. The young sacs are whole and filled with water. Older ones erode at the tips and deflate. Their color ranges from yellowish brown to reddish purple. Sea sac grows on upper to midtidal rocks at Palomarin and Pillar Point. Harvest young plants in late spring and summer for use in tempura.

Stone Hair *(Enteromorpha clathrata)*

This looks a bit like green hair. The mass of strands are very fine, soft, and profusely branched, growing up to 16 inches long. It grows on rocks and on mudflats where fresh water flows into salt water. Found in Bolinas Lagoon near Volunteer Canyon, it can be harvested in early to mid-spring and used like green nori *(Enteromorpha intestinalis)*.

CHAPTER 9

Teas, Seasonings, and Medicinal Plants

*P*icking just enough leaves to make a cup of tea or flavor a stew is one of the most relaxing forms of foraging. You can harvest all you need in approximately 15 seconds. Most leaves don't need to be dried for tea. Just put a few in a cup, fill it with boiling water, and instantly you've got a new flavor and fragrance to enjoy. ✿ The Bay Area climate produces a wonderful variety of strong plant aromas. I have loved experimenting with the fruitily coniferous Douglas fir, bracing yarrow and sagebrush, honey-scented clover, and well-named pineapple weed. One little native mint has such a delightful scent that the Spaniards named it yerba buena—the good herb. And bay trees, whose pungent, spicy leaves are sold in supermarkets, grow here abundantly. ✿ Since I have no reliable way to test the safety and usefulness of most medicinal plants, I've included very few. However, some local plants are gentle, proven sources of mild relief for colds, coughs, or upset stomachs. If they also have fragrances or flavors that I've found pleasing, independent of their usefulness, they are included here. They might give comfort the next time you're laid low. ✿ The only guide I've seen that emphasizes the medicinal uses of local plants is out of print, but your library may have it: *Wild Edible and Medicinal Plants of California* by Jeff Callegari and Keith Durand (El Cerrito: Callegari and Durand, 1977). If you want to pursue this subject, your best bet is probably to consult respected guides to the medicinal uses of North American plants, and then compare the species in them to the local, published floras to see which ones grow here.

Yarrow *(Achillea millefolium)*

Yarrow

Yarrow blooms in late spring and summer, and its bright white flowers contrast strikingly with the brown hills.

The feathery foliage smells wonderful and is used, dried, in tea to relieve cold symptoms. The tea is bitter, but retains the herbal fragrance of the leaves. Yarrow is an astringent; in ancient times, a strong infusion of the leaves was used to slow bleeding from wounds. One source notes that some women skip their periods if they drink the tea two or three days in a row, so go slow with this one. Anything strong enough to do that is likely to affect your body, male or female, in other ways as well.

Where and When to Find It   An unusual variety of habitats throughout the Bay Area supports this common species: wooded, brushy, or open hills; coastal bluffs; and salt-marsh borders.

The plants grow from scratch each year in response to the rains. By March they approach mature size. In late summer and fall, the foliage becomes dry, so collect the leaves earlier.

California or Coastal Sagebrush *(Artemisia californica)*

Sagebrush thrives on steep slopes and rocky ridgetops exposed to the drying effects of wind and sun. Because people are more comfortable living in less exposed settings, sagebrush country stays wild long after more sheltered environments have been built up. The few trees that can grow on the dry sagebrush slopes are widely spaced and, along the coast, severely wind-pruned. In most places where this plant grows, there's nothing above chest height to block the view. The shrub's fresh, powerful fragrance is wedded to long vistas. Sagebrush is the smell of exhilaration after too long in close quarters.

California Sagebrush

The sagebrush that grows in the Bay Area is not the same as the one that dominates America's deserts, *Artemesia tridentata,* although the two smell similar and both have grey-green leaves. The desert sagebrush is bigger and its individual leaves are wider. California sagebrush, the sagebrush of the coastal hills, has leaves like soft needles that grow in clusters along the stems. Its most common close relative in this area is another fragrant *Artemisia,* mugwort.

Nor is sagebrush the same as sage, or even related to it. True sages have the Latin name *Salvia.* Their aromatic leaves have a broader, more common shape, and they are members of the Mint family.

You can prolong the pleasure of smelling sagebrush by using it at home. To make sagebrush tea, put just the tip of a branch in a cup and pour boiling water over it. Within seconds, the water will turn light green and give off a sage aroma; when it does, remove the sagebrush leaves immediately. Tea made this way has a mild bitterness that is more than offset by the superb fragrance; but if the leaves are left to steep too

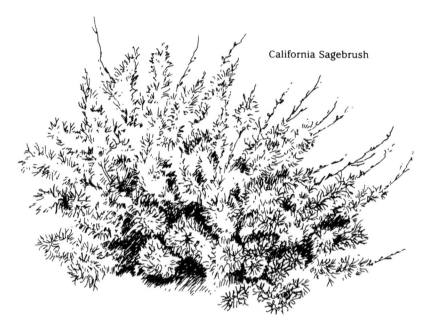

California Sagebrush

long, the brew becomes very bitter. Interestingly, when I seasoned a beef stew with the leaves, allowing them to simmer for quite a while, the stew picked up their herbal flavor without any detectable bitterness. It was delicious.

Where and When to Find It   California sagebrush grows on exposed slopes throughout the Bay Area. It is as at home on the foggy coastal headlands as it is in the hot, dry chaparral of Mt. Diablo. Even in areas where lush redwood groves fill the valleys, the exposed ridges above them usually support sagebrush populations. Wherever you live, you will not need to go far to find it.

The bushes put out fresh growth in November in response to the rains. While you can use it for cooking throughout the year, sagebrush is most appealing during the rainy season. By September and October, the leaves look extremely dry and thin.

Mugwort *(Artemisia douglasiana,* also *A. vulgaris* var. *heterophylla,* and *A. ludoviciana)*

Mugwort is for dreaming. Herbalists use a tea made with its fragrant leaves or its flowers and buds, but mugwort has greater charms to offer. A legend passed down from medieval times holds that sleeping amidst the aroma of these leaves causes us to dream about our future.

The scent is certainly evocative. Crushing a leaf releases an aroma reminiscent of sagebrush, to which mugwort is related, but the fragrance is more complex than sagebrush's clean, straightforward smell. Mugwort leaves, like yarrow, pull at the dim edges of people's memories. Their odor is familiar and haunting. Smelling them is like entering a dark woods that I feel I've seen before, even though I can't think when and perhaps saw only in a dream.

This is a bitter herb. Its English sibling, wormwood *(Artemisia absinthium)* is the second bitterest herb known, after rue, and was used to flavor absinthe liqueur. Mugwort was used in Europe to give the bitter flavor to beer before hops were grown for that purpose. Its leaves have also served to repel moths from wool clothing.

Mugwort

Each year, mugwort grows from scratch into a plant several feet tall, usually with the leaves growing attached to a single straight stem. The leaves of most mugworts are grey-green with a milky look. The plants grow in colonies; you'll generally see at least four or five together.

Officially, wormwood (which doesn't grow here) is the *Artemisia* that should be used for predictive dreams. You are supposed to mix the leaves with other natural substances and recite a verse before sleeping on them. However, our local mugwort, used without benefit of poetry or ritual, seems to work well enough.

When a friend and I decided to try sleeping on some leaves, we gathered them from plants that were well developed but still green all over. Each of us pinched off the tips from about six plants, enough to concentrate the fragrance, and tucked them in our pillowcases that night.

My friend, an accomplished artist, is a single woman in her thirties who looks forward to having a family someday. In her dream that night, she was climbing a high mountain and holding her young son in her arms. She wore a long, black cloak and was carrying him inside of it, bundled against the mountain winds. As she walked, she played a game with the baby, asking him riddles for which the correct answer was "Daddy." The child's father, her husband, was waiting at the top of the mountain, and she was hoping the boy would say "Daddy" when they reached him.

When they made it to the summit, the child delighted both parents by calling "Daddy" quite clearly. They all stood together, gazing at the beautiful vistas before them.

Below them lay the Valley of Home, green and fertile, and beyond it rose the Mountain of Contentment. My friend stood there and drank in the peacefulness of loving her husband and child so deeply. But there was a riddle in the view, a question posed. Next to the green and forested Mountain of Contentment, she remembers a Mountain of Solitude, home to those who pursue their work and dreams alone. Mists hung over its craggy, granite surface, and few plants clung to its slopes. It was a majestic peak, very beautiful and inviting in its own way. The question was, to which would she be going, which mountain would be her home?

Despite its ambiguity, hers was a dream that could only further mugwort's reputation. She woke well pleased with the plant's work. I was not so sure.

My dream was set a number of years in the future. In it, my sister and I had waited so long to have children, while we pieced together our careers, that we had finally driven our mother to irrationality on the subject. Normally a reasonable person, she could no longer bear the questioning, pitying eyes of her friends who were enjoying youthful grandparenthood.

She decided that my sister and I must publish a declaration in the birth announcements section of the local paper. In it we would state that, although we were not yet ready to start families, we did in fact love babies very much and were definitely looking forward to having children someday.

My sister and I spent the rest of the dream trying to persuade her of the confusion and misinterpretation this would lead to, but she was adamant.

I awoke reminded of what a great blessing it is that we are not burdened with knowledge of the future. However, if you are undissuaded and want to expose yourself to the enigmas and revelations this plant evokes, you can find it throughout the Bay Area.

It's always bad magic to destroy life unnecessarily, so don't uproot whole plants. Be artful. Pick a leaf here and a leaf there until you have enough, and chances are that your labors will be unnoticeable. Or in a large clump, carefully pinch off the top 6 inches or so of stem and leaves from several plants. If you pinch a stem right above a spot where leaves are attached, the plant will look much better than if you leave a long, bare stem tip exposed. The leaves are so fragrant that you won't need many. An acquaintance who took a large quantity found their smell so powerful that she couldn't fall asleep on them.

Where and When to Find It   Mugwort is one of those agreeable plants that frequents much of the Bay Area and grows in a wide variety of habitats. It favors moist places, such as streambanks, dried streambeds, and shady or north-facing slopes. It also grows on grassy hillsides and in the open chaparral of the headlands. As examples, I've seen goodly amounts of mugwort in Tennessee Valley in the GGNRA and at Las Trampas Regional Park, on the slope up to Rocky Ridge. Once you can recognize it, you'll see mugwort on a majority of the hikes you take in this area.

The time to gather the leaves is roughly from March through September, though March may be too early for the plants in some locations, and September may be too late for others. When the rains begin in late autumn, a new crop of mugwort begins to grow, but it does not reach its mature size until March, April, or May, depending on the climate in a particular year and location. Gathering leaves before the plants are full-grown is wasteful; the larger the leaves are, the fewer plants you must disturb to get enough of the fragrance to alter your dreams.

By September, many lower leaves will be dry and buff colored. However, the tips will still be green and aromatic. Mugwort gathered in late summer has had an opportunity to flower and go to seed, a strong argument in favor of waiting until then.

Mexican Tea or Epazote *(Chenopodium ambrosioides)*

This sibling of lamb's quarters is intensely aromatic and is used, fresh or dried, in cooking. In southern France, Germany, the West Indies, and Mexico, the dried leaves are brewed to make a tea. In Mexican and Guatemalan cuisine, epazote is an essential ingredient in black-bean recipes, and is also used to season corn, mushroom, fish, and shellfish dishes.

Diana Kennedy, an authority on Mexican cookery, strongly recommends that epazote be used fresh. In New York, she can gather it in Central and Riverside parks. It grows as a weed here, as well.

Epazote stands from 2 to 4 feet tall. Its leaves look very similar to those of lamb's quarters, except that their undersides are not mealy

white and they are powerfully aromatic. One source describes the smell as varnishlike. Kennedy calls it "very much an acquired taste."

Where and When to Find It
To be honest, this is not the easiest weed to find. I never have. You may need to start your own patch of it from seed, in some appropriately weedy spot. Epazote is found occasionally in disturbed areas and grasslands.

At one time or another, it has been seen at Crystal Springs, Menlo Park, and Stanford on the

Mexican Tea

Peninsula; at Sausalito, the Rock Spring area of Mt. Tam, Stinson Beach, and Ignacio in Marin; at the Presidio, Lands End, Golden Gate Park, Pine Lake, and Lake Merced in San Francisco; and at Point Pinole and Coyote Hills in the East Bay.

Epazote looks lushest and most attractive during the rainy season, but all the water alters its flavor. Plants gathered in the summer have a more characteristic taste.

Yerba Santa *(Eriodictyon californicum)*

This native shrub has very shiny, leathery, often sticky leaves with a unique, refreshing fragrance. To smell it, rub a leaf between your fingers. Chewing a leaf is an old tradition said to produce a bitter, resinous taste followed by a sweet, cooling sensation, particularly after you stop chewing or drink some water. I have always found a drink of water to be a relief after chewing a leaf. On the other hand, I do like to suck gently on a yerba santa leaf. So long as I don't bite it and release the bitterness, holding one in my mouth releases its enjoyable mixture of resin and fragrance.

As a medicinal tea, yerba santa is renowned for the relief it can bring to people with congested chests

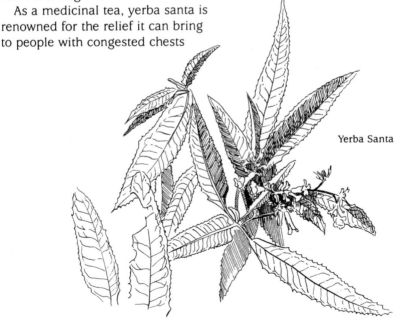

Yerba Santa

due to colds. The *U.S. Pharmacopoeia* has recognized the leaves as being helpful in "chronic subacute inflammation of the bronchial tubes."

The tea is bitter and should be brewed strong to be effective. Try boiling the dried leaves in water with some honey, rather than just pouring the boiling water over them. This approach is supposed to improve the flavor.

If you aren't sick and just want to enjoy the fragrance of this plant, try making tea by pouring boiling water over one leaf only. The flavor will be mild and the aroma soothing.

Where and When to Find It Yerba santa is a conspicuous shrub in brushy areas and chaparral because of the dark shininess of its leaves. It grows from 2 to 8 feet tall. It is particularly common where chaparral has burned or been cleared (for example, along fire roads). You'll find it on sunny, dry ridges inland from the immediate coast. So, for example, in Mt. Tamalpais State Park, it grows along the Deer Park Fire Road, from which you can see the ocean shining in the distance below, but it does not appear on the headlands adjacent to the water. Yerba santa is not a grassland species.

The plant occurs sparingly in the western part of the East Bay in such places as Sobrante Ridge, Manzanita Grove, the Huckleberry Preserve area, and Flicker Ridge. Inland, toward Black Diamond Mines Regional Park and Mt. Diablo, it becomes common. In Marin and on the Peninsula, explore the ridgeline fire roads and you'll find it without much difficulty.

Many of the leaves become blackened with a disease as they mature, so the easiest time to find clean leaves is in March, April, and May, while the new ones are still fresh. However, at least a few clean ones can be found year round. And the shrubs always smell good, even when most of the leaves are smutty.

Yerba Santa

Blue Gum Eucalyptus *(Eucalyptus globulus)*

People seem either to love the fragrance of these trees or to hate it. Whichever camp you fall in, you may find the long, curving leaves of the blue gum (the most common species here) useful when you have a head cold. A cup of tea made with two leaves, fresh or dried, will help clear your head. The leaves are available for tea-making the year round. The tea should also help with a cough; Halls cough drops contain eucalyptus oil. If you want to try making your own eucalyptus cough drops, adapting the recipe on page 189 should work.

Blue Gum
Eucalyptus

I have read that fleas are repelled by the smell of the leaves and nuts, and that one can drive them out of a home by spreading the leaves around for a time. This sounds messy, but if you have kids, they would probably think it was fun and you would avoid the need for chemicals.

Originally, eucalyptus were brought here from Australia as part of a failed lumber speculation. The speculator didn't discover until harvest time that the Australians use other species of eucalyptus for lumber and that the blue gums he'd planted were worthless for that purpose. Meanwhile, besides losing all the money he'd convinced people to invest in eucalyptus groves, he had dramatically altered the character of the East Bay hills.

Since then, blue gums have made themselves rather too much at home throughout the Bay Area. They have few natural enemies here and formidable resilience. Because the original trees were brought here as seeds, the insects

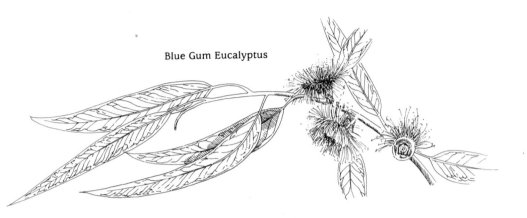

Blue Gum Eucalyptus

that attack mature trees in Australia did not come along. So our blue gums tend to be more vigorous than their Australian counterparts.

Once a eucalyptus is established anywhere, it has an impressive variety of mechanisms for staying alive. Young trees have a swelling just below the soil surface called a lignotuber. If the main trunk is destroyed by fire or grazing, the lignotuber produces a thicket of sprouts to replace it. Trees of all ages have buds hidden under the bark along the trunk and branches, so that if the crown of the tree is destroyed these buds can put out new branches. This characteristic makes radical tree surgery possible. On our street in the city, crews come once every three years and cut off the entire branch system of the eucalyptus street trees to keep them from tangling in the wires above. The trees are left as ugly wooden poles with bark on them, but within half a year, the trunks sprout a ball of new branches. As another line of regenerative defense, each leaf has at its base a second bud, held in readiness in case harm comes to the first leaf. If a fire scorches all the leaves or a drought shrivels them, the tree simply replaces them as soon as conditions return to normal.

Eucalyptus are detested by some as a messy, shedding species that crowds out native vegetation. They have nonetheless become an institution here, and many of us consider their penetrating aroma a basic element in the catalogue of smells that add up to "home."

Where and When to Find It   You can harvest leaves for tea any time of the year. I doubt there is a community in the entire Bay Area that does not have these trees. Ask anyone who's lived here a while to point one out to you.

Horehound *(Marrubium vulgare)*

Horehound

Whenever my sister, brothers, or I were laid low with a childhood illness that included nausea, our southern pediatrician prescribed Coca Cola. It always helped. The cola soothed the spasms and the sugary fizz lifted our spirits. A generation earlier, children with persistent coughs or sore throats were given horehound candies or horehound syrup, and I imagine the treatment always helped them, too.

Horehound has the square stems that indicate membership in the Mint family, but its whitish green, woolly leaves taste bitter, not minty. The plants grow up to 3 feet tall and are usually found in colonies of at least several individuals.

Where and When to Find It   Horehound is widely distributed and relatively common in the Bay Area. It is found along roads and in waste ground. According to the botanists, horehound is common in Marin and on the Peninsula, but is only occasional in the East Bay. However, I've come across more of it in the East Bay than elsewhere. Also, I've usually found it near water, although the descriptions of its habitat do not indicate such a pattern.

The best place to learn to identify this species is at Sunol Regional Park, because a large patch of it grows next to the interpretive center. The naturalists can easily point it out to you. I've also seen smaller patches at Coyote Hills, S.F. Bay National Wildlife Refuge, Palo Alto Baylands, Tennessee Valley, and along the Panoramic Highway in Marin. Even though this is an introduced species, you would still need a ranger's permission to pick horehound in any of the parks.

HOREHOUND SYRUP OR COUGH DROPS

To make syrup or cough drops, begin by simmering 1 cup of leaves in a pint of water for 10 minutes. Let the mixture sit for another 5 minutes, then strain out the leaves.

For syrup: measure the liquid and mix in twice as much honey.

For cough drops: add 2 cups of sugar to the liquid, along with a teaspoon of butter. If you have a candy thermometer, heat the mixture until it reaches 290° F.

Without a thermometer, you will need to drip a drop into a glass of cold water periodically. When the drop instantly forms a hard, round ball upon hitting the water, remove the mixture from the heat.

Around 220°, the mixture will froth up to about four times its original volume, so use a saucepan that is sufficiently deep. Just when you think it will surely overflow, it sinks back down and foams quietly in the bottom of the pot. Do not stir the mixture once the ingredients have melted and become blended; stirring will only slow the process. At about 270° to 280°, it will begin to darken, and by 290°, the brew is a rich, dark brown.

Pour the 290° candy into a well-buttered cookie sheet with an inch-high rim. When it has cooled to a semisolid, score it with a knife, marking off rectangles in whatever size you want the final pieces to be. When the candy (or cough drops) has completely cooled, it will break easily along those lines. Store in a dry place.

When the sugar and horehound infusion first start heating, the blend is terribly bitter, but somewhere along the temperature scale, a harmony develops in the flavors, so that the resulting candies are deliciously bittersweet.

The plants come up fresh and full in response to the rains. From mid-November through the winter and spring, they are at their best. In the dry season, the lower leaves drop off, although the tips stay green through the fall.

Pineapple Weed *(Matricaria matricarioides)*
Chamomile, Mayweed, or Dog Fennel
(Anthemis cotula)

These two plants are our nearest equivalents to true chamomile, which is *Anthemis nobilis,* and to German or Hungarian chamomile, which is *Matricaria chamomilla.*

Mayweed looks like true chamomile. Its small flowers have dome-shaped, yellow centers and a ring of white petals. The leaves are lacy. The plants are low growing, usually less than a foot tall.

Its leaves have a strong odor, which some people consider pungent and others dislike. Both the leaves and flowers, when dried, can be used to make tea, but some herbalists recommend using only the yellow flowers, after plucking off most of the white petals. Mayweed tea has been listed in the *U.S. Pharmacopoeia* as an aid in relieving colic and menstrual cramps. You will find the flavor bitter, compared to that of true chamomile tea.

Pineapple weed does indeed smell like pineapples, and tea made with the leaves and flowers, fresh or dried, is not bitter. The pineapple

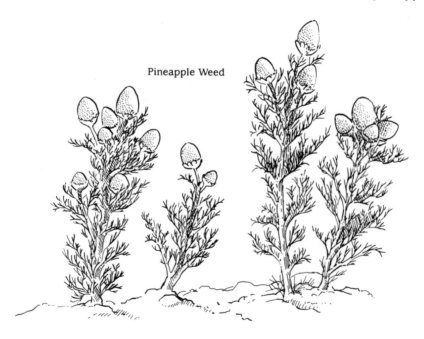

Pineapple Weed

fragrance is greatly enhanced if you leave the flowers in the tea while you drink it. A trace of sugar also helps bring out the flavor. This is one of the most easily likable wild teas we have.

The very low-growing plants rarely exceed 6 inches in height. However, they are easy to spot because of their bright, greenish yellow, domed flowers, which have no petals.

Where and When to Find Them Mayweed, a European native, is most often found in grazing lands, but also grows in waste ground. In Marin, San Francisco, and on the Peninsula, it is common and widespread. In the East Bay, it is most abundant in the Tassajara Park area, north of Livermore.

This annual can be found blooming all year, but flowers most heavily in late spring and early summer.

Chamomile

Pineapple weed specializes in hard-packed dirt. In towns, it appears in sidewalk cracks and at the base of street trees, but neither of those make appetizing collection sites. In parks, it grows right up the center of dirt fire roads in sunny locations.

I've seen lots of pineapple weed on dirt roads in the following locations: below Inspiration Point in the Presidio of San Francisco, on the hills of Garin Ranch Regional Park above Hayward, and in Mitchell Canyon at Mt. Diablo. But these are just examples; you'll find it in many other places, as well. It is very common on the Peninsula; occasional in Marin, mostly near towns; and widespread though not particularly common in the East Bay.

The flowers first appear in February and March, but on many plants the pineapple aroma is stronger in April, May, and June.

WILD MINTS

Native:

Field or Marsh Mint *(Mentha arvensis)*
Coyote Mint or Western Pennyroyal
(Monardella villosa)
Yerba Buena *(Satureja chamissonis)*

Introduced:

Bergamot Mint *(Mentha citrata)*
Peppermint *(M. piperita)*
Pennyroyal *(M. pulegium)*
Apple Mint *(M. rotundifolia)*
Spearmint *(M. spicata)*

One summer afternoon, my husband and I were hiking in the Sierra and sat down to rest. A wonderfully refreshing mint aroma filled the air. We looked all around us to find the plant responsible, and finally realized that he was sitting on a clump of pennyroyal. That was our introduction to the wild mints of California. Once we discovered pennyroyal in that way, we noticed it often along the trail. Chewing on an occasional leaf added greatly to the pleasure of the hike.

The Bay Area is also rich in mints; once you recognize them, you'll be able to find a leaf to crush or chew on most hikes. We have woodland mints, field mints, and mints for dry hillsides. Each species has its own character and charm.

While the plants are usually largest and fullest in late spring or summer, most of the mints are available year round.

The Natives

Field or **marsh mint** has a powerful odor and flavor, best for sniffing as you walk. It is an occasional member of coastal marshes and pond margins on the Peninsula and in Marin. It blooms from August through October.

Coyote mint can be easily distinguished from the other local mints when it is blooming. It has a single flower at the top of each stem, rather than a stack of round blossoms like all of the Mentha species. Its spicy

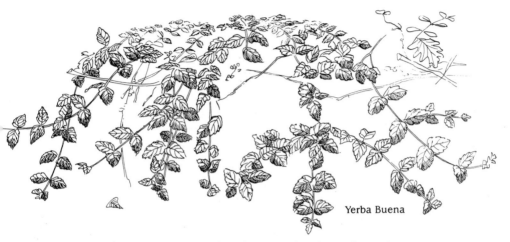

Yerba Buena

leaves are fairly common on brushy or rocky slopes from the coast to Mt. Diablo. One hot afternoon when I was lost in Las Trampas with a friend, the discovery of a clump of coyote mint did wonders for our spirits. We sat and sniffed leaves until we could face the rest of the scratchy, free-form descent through the scrub. Coyote mint blooms from May through September.

Yerba buena (meaning "good herb") was the original name that the Spaniards gave to San Francisco. They named it for the trailing mint that once was common here. Outside of the city, yerba buena is still a frequent sight along the edges of hiking trails. It is common from the coast inland to Briones, but is rare on Mt. Diablo. It grows in forests, in brush, and on open, coastal hills.

More so than the other mints, this one changes its fragrance seasonally. In February and March, the new leaves unfold. They are softer and lighter than the ones that wintered on the plant. Through the spring, the new leaves have a fruity, lemony fragrance, blended with the mintiness. By June, they lose that quality and smell traditionally minty. As a wild tea, the spring leaves are particularly outstanding. The small, white blossoms appear from May through August.

Introduced Species

Bergamot mint has become established in Palo Alto, Muir Beach, Stinson Beach, Mill Valley, and several San Francisco parks. The leaves contain a lemon-scented oil used in perfumes and in the liqueur Chartreuse. The flowers, which bloom from July through October, smell like lavendar.

Peppermint makes an occasional showing along urban streams in the East Bay and near Alviso. It is the traditional mint used to flavor sweet foods and beverages. Peppermint blooms from August through November.

Pennyroyal

Pennyroyal grows in gratifying abundance in the right circumstances. For example, in Tennessee Valley in Marin, it fills the ditches and low fields for half a mile. This European native is common throughout the Bay Area in low areas that are marshy all winter but dry in summer. These include roadside ditches, low fields, and vernal pools, especially where livestock graze. Small clumps also grow along streams occasionally.

The leaves smell strongly spearminty and are good, fresh or dried, in stuffings or other savory dishes. I made some pennyroyal tea in winter, and though it was fragrant, the marshy ditch where it had grown was present in the flavor. The leaves might taste better if picked in summer or fall.

In late summer and fall, pennyroyal blooms in tiers of pom-pom-like flowers colored a stunning deep lavendar purple. Where it grows in solid patches, the effect is quite beautiful.

Spearmint

Apple mint is listed in the floras as having been noticed only at Boulder Creek and the Mill Valley marshes. Its leaves do have an apple-like aroma, and it blooms from July through September.

Spearmint is the most popular domestic mint and makes a delicious tea. It has become naturalized in the fog-zone parks of San Francisco and occasionally appears in other wet places or stream banks near human dwellings. For example, this mint has been found at Stanford, the Mill Valley marshes, Bolinas, and Mitchell Canyon on Mt. Diablo.

I have found a few plants hidden under a bush at Lands End in San Francisco, and usually pick a leaf to crush or chew whenever I pass them. It's satisfying to crawl in under the branches and see that my secret mint garden is still doing well. Spearmint blooms from July through October.

Douglas Fir Forest

Douglas Fir *(Pseudotsuga menziesii)*

Some chill, foggy summer day when you are hiking through a coastal forest, gently pinch some twigs off a Douglas fir. (It will grow back more fully next year, in the places where you prune it back.) At home afterward, with mist swirling past your windows and fir tea warming you, the coziness and fragrance of winter can be yours, a full six months ahead of time.

This is my favorite wild tea because we used fir trees as Christmas trees when I was a child. Smells can jog memories from a time even before we could talk, and inhaling the aroma of Douglas fir tea always brings me images of Christmas as simple and exciting as a toddler's fantasies: firelight and candlelight, time with my family, special foods, bright packages, and prayers for snow. See what it conjures up for you.

The trees are easy to identify. In the Bay Area, the needle-bearing trees you see will usually be Douglas firs or redwoods. Douglas firs have needles growing out in all directions from the twigs, and their grey trunks are often covered with grey-green lichens and moss. Redwoods have needles going out in a flat layer from the twigs, and they have the trademark reddish bark. Redwood tea is also safe to drink, by the way, but it smells more like weak oyster broth than like a fir forest.

Using needles alone, you might conceivably confuse Douglas firs with the much less common California nutmegs (also known as Pacific yews), and since the fruit of the nutmeg is poisonous, it would be a bad idea to try the needles (which are very sharp). It's rare to see a nutmeg in most woods around here, and once you've seen a few Douglas firs, you'll easily be able to tell the two apart. But in the beginning, to be positive that a tree is a Douglas fir, find one of its cones. If the cone has slender, three-pointed tails hanging down all over it, you've found the right tree.

To make the tea, just pinch off a couple of sprigs from the tips of branches, put them in a cup, add boiling water, and let them sit a few minutes. By the time the tea is cool enough to drink, it will have a faint, semisweet, semiresinous taste and a wonderful aroma. For a large mug, you'll need two or three sprigs, each about 4 or 5 inches long.

Some people think the tea is best when made from the fresh, new branchlets that cover the firs in April, May, and June. As summer and fall progress, the new growth becomes darker, until by November it matches the dark green of the older needles. I compared new-growth tea and mature twig tea and preferred the tea made with older, darker needles. They tasted about the same, but the fir fragrance was much stronger from the tea of the mature needles.

Where and When to Find It   The outer coast range is prime Douglas fir terrain; the tallest tree in Muir Woods is not a redwood but a Douglas fir! They grow in the Rockies and the Sierra as well, but are tallest along the West Coast. You will find them in both the Marin and Peninsula forests. The forest at Point Reyes is mostly Douglas fir. Firs need fog to thrive. In the East Bay they grow only in the limited fog belt and even there only if they've been planted. The needles are available year round.

Douglas Fir

White Clover *(Trifolium repens)*
Red Clover *(T. pratense)*

The taste and aroma of clover blossom tea remind me of honey, undoubtedly because most commercial honeybees gather their nectar in clover fields. To make this pleasing brew, dry red or white clover blossoms in a low oven (200° F. or lower) for 15 to 20 minutes, or until they feel bone dry to the touch. Then put five or more blossoms in a cup, fill it with boiling water, and let the tea steep, covered, for at least 5 minutes. The tea will have more fragrance if you leave the blossoms in the cup while you drink it.

Both the leaves and blossoms of white clover can be cooked as vegetables. Either soak them in salty water and then steam them for 10 minutes or avoid the soaking step by boiling them in salty water for 10 minutes. The exposure to salt reduces clover's tendency to cause bloating. The cooked flowers taste like artichokes or broccoli. The leaves (minus their tough stems) are a little chewy, but taste good.

White Clover

Where and When to Find

Them White and red clover are only two of many local clover species. They grow in rich, moist, lightly disturbed soils. Look for them in lawns, meadows, and grazed pasturelands. The white clover can be found throughout the Bay Area. Red clover is rare in Marin, but does grow on the Peninsula and in the East Bay.

The leaves are available most of the year. The blossoms appear between April and October, depending on the location.

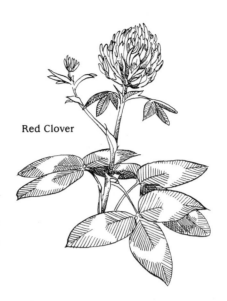

Red Clover

California Bay, California Laurel, or Bay Laurel
(Umbellularia californica)

On the spice shelves in supermarkets you can find jars marked "California Bay Leaves" and buy them for use in cooking. Or you can pick them for free on your next hike.

Bay leaves. We cook with them so often, adding their spicy aroma to stews, soups, pot roasts, and tomato sauces. How pleasant it is to be able to pick our own in woods all over the Bay Area! I love to pinch off a leaf and enjoy its fragrance as I walk along a trail. Hold them at least a few inches from your face. Before I knew better, I crushed them right under my nose to get a full whiff. The strong oils exploded in my sinuses, with the same sensation as getting water up my nose when swimming.

Bay trees are easiest to identify by using your nose. If you study the smell of a commercial bay leaf, you will easily recognize the same odor in the woods. The dark green leaves are several inches long and thin. They have a prominent vein up the center, are smooth edged, and are rather tough.

The trees often cluster together in groves, particularly along streams and on the steep slopes above them. They always grow directly up toward the light; if one falls over but remains alive, its branches on the sky side will thicken and develop into a row of mini-trees. A bay grove is a grey-green, somewhat mysterious place. The trees grow so densely that the light is heavily filtered and there's little undergrowth. Add a few Douglas firs with their licheny bark, a twisted live oak, and some giant ferns, and you have the classic California coastal forest—a setting made for fairy tales.

Our native bay leaves are more aromatic than the ones usually sold for cooking, *Laurus nobilis* from the Mediterranean and redbay from our Atlantic and Gulf coasts. Authorities on wild-food plants generally suggest using half as much California bay as you would of other bay leaves. However, most cookbooks are so timid about seasonings that I've had no trouble using them in the amounts called for.

The old way to dry bay leaves for use in cooking was to break off a branch, tie it upside down in a dry spot, and pick off the leaves when they were ready. However, one era's acceptable behavior becomes another era's vandalism. Rather than taking a branch, simply pick as many mature leaves as you need, spread them out on a flat surface covered with a paper towel, and let them dry for a few days before putting them in an airtight container. Remember that all herbs lose flavor with time, and your food will taste better if you prepare a fresh supply of bay leaves at least once a year. I like to bring home 10 or 12 leaves, which I can dry on a plate without making a big production of it. Those last me a few months and then I harvest another pocketful.

Some people make beautiful wreaths of bay laurel leaves for winter holiday decorations and then enjoy them in their kitchens the rest of the year, gradually using up the leaves for cooking. The ancient Greeks also thought laurel wreaths were lovely and made them into garlands for victorious athletes; because of that custom, the word laurels has become a synonym for praise and honors.

The leaves have another useful property in addition to their flavor. Quite simply, insects hate their smell. You can use this to your advantage when you want to keep flies away from a picnic or from food near an open window; just put a few leaves around the dishes. If your cat or dog has fleas, scattering bay leaves around the yard is said to drive them away. Alternately, stringing a few leaves onto a pet's collar should also do the trick, if the animal's sensitive nose can stand it.

Insect-repellant properties are fine in a plant until it needs to reproduce. Then there's a conflict. Bays, like most advanced plants, bloom and then need insects to carry pollen from one flower to the ovaries of

California Bay

another flower, thereby fertilizing it so that a new bay nut can grow, drop off, and start a new bay tree. But as long as the bugs can smell the leaves, they avoid the trees.

Perhaps bays could have evolved to avoid this problem by spreading their pollen on the wind. Fortunately for us, they went another route. Their flowers developed a jasmine fragrance so powerful that when a branch is in full bloom, the odor of the leaves is completely masked.

The trees can start blooming as soon as the end of November in a year with early rains, along the ridges near the coast. By January, most trees, even in the colder East Bay, have some blossoms open. But a warm mid-February day is by far the best time to smell them. Walk along trails on still, sunny days and as you enter a grove of bay trees, the fragrance will fill the air.

If you go a little too early, or on a cold day, or walk in a shady place, you will be able to smell the flowers only by putting your nose right up to them. I've had the best luck in East Bay parks where the trail led through a sunny hillside grove or along a broad valley where the trees received lots of warmth. One great spot is in Briones Park on the Abrigo Valley Trail, just beyond the Bear Creek entrance and picnic area.

In late summer, you will begin to see hard, green fruits on the bays. By October, they are ripe all over the Bay Area, and the green fruit becomes soft and darkens to a purple color. At that point, the fruit is edible, with a taste and texture somewhat similar to avocado. After the bay fruits fall to the ground, the soft exterior rots away, exposing a hard nut inside. The Indians used to eat roasted bay nuts with meals and on strenuous journeys, comparing them to our coffee.

The nuts are full of pungent oils. Biting into a raw one is like biting into a fresh bay leaf—extremely strong tasting. Just as insects avoid the leaves, the usual nut-eating creatures seem to avoid the nuts. I was able to collect several dozen in December, after they'd been on the ground several months, and when I got them cleaned and shelled, I was amazed to see that not one had any worm holes or bugs or blemishes of any kind. In that respect, at least, they are a forager's dream food. Their shells come off easily, revealing two pale green halves. Try baking the shelled nuts at 350° F. for about half an hour until they are a rich brown color and crunchy. The baking modifies their bitterness and makes it not only bearable but also mildly interesting. Taste them in small bits.

I had notions of leaching out the bitterness, baking them until they were dry, and producing a delicacy, but this failed. The first two changes of boiling water turned a very unnatural (though beautiful) pale aquamarine, the third bath turned forest green, and in the end the nuts were just as bitter as before and mushy. Stick to baking them.

Where and When to Find It   Bay trees are obligingly common. Their natural range is the entire California and Oregon coast and the Sierra Nevada. In the Bay Area, you will find them in most forests, except in the most eastern areas, such as Black Diamond Mines and the region northeast of Mt. Diablo. Trees along streams bear more nuts than ridgetop bays.

The blooming period is normally from December through March, but mid-February is definitely the time to visit a bay grove if you want the full effect of their fragrance. Those questionable nuts can be harvested from at least October through mid-winter. Best of all, the leaves are available year round.

See also
Blackberry Leaves, page 57
Bladderwrack, page 159
Elderberry Blossoms, page 60
Fennel Seeds, page 112
Madrone Bark, page 38
Rose Hips, page 53
Strawberry Leaves, page 44

CHAPTER 10

Trail Nibbles

*T*he plants in this section produce foods that are too small and insignificant to harvest for cooking but that add dimension to a hike. Sometimes it bothers me that I'm so physically isolated from the landscapes I walk in. My shoes cut me off from the feel of the trail, and unless I make a point of reaching out to touch bark or leaves as I pass, there's no contact at all between my body and the land. ✿ The flower buds, fruits, and seeds included here have helped me feel more connected. It's easier to feel I've been in a place with my whole self (not just my mind, eyes, and leg muscles) if I've tasted and swallowed some tiny part of the place. So I keep my eyes open for these miniature tidbits and am grateful when I have the chance to nibble as well as look and listen.

Ocean Spray or Cream Bush *(Holodiscus discolor)*

This shrub can grow up to 12 feet tall in canyons and on the north-facing slopes it prefers. The flowers bloom in attractive sprays of creamy blossoms at the tips of the branches. In leaf texture and size, it resembles hazelnut, which grows in the same places. But hazelnut has very different flowers: the female ones are solitary at stem joints, and the males are long, slender tassels with no petals.

As a trail nibble, the greenish flower buds of ocean spray are refreshing. They taste like thyme—herby, strong, and a little bitter. A few tiny buds are ample to enjoy the flavor; more would be unpleasant. After all, if you were going to chew thyme leaves straight, you wouldn't fill your mouth with them.

Where and When to Find It   The flowers bloom in May and June, and May is the best time to find plenty of buds. After flowering, the dried seed husks remain on the bushes most of the year. You'll see them from July through early spring hanging in conspicuous, brown clusters.

Ocean spray is widespread and common in Marin, on the Peninsula, and in the East Bay all the way to Mt. Diablo. It grows in oak and fir forests, along streams, and in soft chaparral. If you hike on a north-facing slope, you'll probably pass it in almost any Bay Area park. Would that all wild edibles were so obliging.

Ocean Spray

Peppergrass

Peppergrass *(Lepidium nitidum)*

Peppergrass thrives on the green hills of late winter and early spring. The plant and its setting are perfect foils for each other: the one so hot and sharp to the taste, and the other so immensely soft and gentle to the gaze.

This diminutive member of the Mustard family grows about 3 to 4 inches high. In late winter and spring, it develops small seedpods, flattish discs with a line down their centers. The pods are arranged loosely at the top of a very slender stalk, and are quite edible. They start out green, turning red as they mature. By the time they are fully red, they are often dry. The pods taste best when their tops have turned red but their undersides are still green.

Finding peppergrass is not the easiest sort of foraging. When the pods are solid green, the plants blend so well with surrounding grass that you may miss them, even if you are walking past hundreds of them. The deep red color helps them stand out, but even that does not make them obvious. Until your eyes become accustomed to picking them out, you will need to stop every now and then on likely trails and take a hard look at the small plants at your feet. As is so often the case, spotting peppergrass the second time is much simpler than when you've never seen it growing.

Peppergrass is one of my favorite wild foods in the nibbling category. Abundant along grassy trails, the small seedpods have just enough radishy bite to be irresistible.

If you wanted to use the seedpods in meals, they might taste good in a vegetable or meat dish, and would certainly enhance a salad. I've never brought any home to try with other foods. For me, they are the quintessential trail food, meant to be eaten as I walk. It's a game to try to spot them along the path, and another game to try to position them, tiny as they are, between my teeth. The rewards are a burst of vivid flavor and the pleasure of engaging my hands and taste buds in exploring a landscape.

Where and When to Find It   You will find peppergrass most easily along the trails that follow the ridgetops where cows graze. Because it is not a native, it grows more commonly in disturbed areas than in wilderness. It can handle very disturbed areas. I saw one hardy clump poking through a crack in the sidewalk at a busy San Francisco intersection. Short of a toxic waste dump, that must be one of the ultimate macho locations for a plant. It was growing flat against the pavement and was covered with healthy-looking seedpods. Out in foraging country, I have seen peppergrass most often in the East Bay Regional Parks on little-used dirt roads leading through large grassy areas.

The pods are ripe from late February through April. The usual rule that plants develop later away from the coast does not seem to apply in this case. I have seen it ripe by early March in Briones and Las Trampas (try on Rocky Ridge). Out on the headlands, it continues in its prime through April, and in wet years, into May.

Shepherd's Purse *(Capsella bursa-pastoris)*

This little member of the Mustard family is similar to peppergrass in almost every respect except the shape of its seedpods. Each pod is heart shaped, so the stems are quite appealing, with all the tiny hearts attached to them. This plant got its common name because the seedpods were thought to resemble the purses that shepherds once carried.

Like peppergrass, the seedpods have a pleasant, radishy taste, are most common in disturbed grasslands and grazed areas, and ripen from January through April.

I have read that the Indians used the leaves as a vegetable, but they are so tiny that it is hard to imagine collecting enough to make a dish of them. Perhaps they were used more to flavor other greens than as a vegetable in their own right.

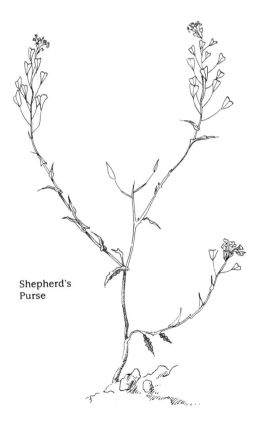

Shepherd's
Purse

A tea made of the dried pods and stems is sold in some health-food stores. My husband thought his cupful tasted and smelled like a cross between seaweed tea and hay. If the constant excitement of living in the Bay Area has left you hankering for something bland, dull, and mediocre, then shepherd's purse tea would delight you. Otherwise, I'd recommend nibbling it raw as you hike, and leaving it at that.

Where and When to Find It Shepherd's purse is common all over the Bay Area—on the Peninsula, and in Marin, the East Bay, and the Delta. It grows in city parks in San Francisco as well as it does in remote valleys.

It's small and wispy, blending in well with green grass, so you may not find it easily at first. Look for it at the edges of dirt and gravel parking lots at trailheads, in fields if you go to a U-pick farm, along dirt paths through parks where cows graze (such as Briones, Las Trampas, or Mt. Diablo), or in sunny, run-down corners of city parks. For example, at the parking area and trailhead for Briones Reservoir on the EBMUD lands, shepherd's purse grows in healthy clumps, coming up amidst the gravel and packed dirt. I've also seen a few plants in Mountain Lake Park in San Francisco, growing in poor, dry soil where grass never did well.

In early spring, whenever you are near cows or in a spot with that neglected, vacant-lot appearance, look for short stems with little hearts attached. Sooner or later, you'll find them.

Australian Saltbush *(Atriplex semibaccata)*

This is a plant for people who are determined to taste every edible species in the Bay Area. Someday, you may happen upon this utterly unassuming little plant, and then its tiny fruits will add that extra pleasure to your walk that only a wild nibble can give.

You will find Australian saltbush on dry, salty soil or near salt marshes. Unlike some of its relatives, which really are bush sized, Australian saltbush grows only a few inches high, sprawling instead over the ground. The leaves are grey-green, so the minuscule but red fruits stand out.

I found ripe saltbush fruits on a dike at Grizzly Island in Suisun Marsh. It was September, and the dike was in full sun, so the plants were covered with dust. However, the fruits were readily visible. If you've been waiting long enough to taste a plant, you don't quibble about a little dust when you find it.

Australian Saltbush

The fruits are about the size of very small huckleberries. Some say they taste like tomatoes. Perhaps they do. I found them slightly tart, or acidic, but otherwise nondescript. Tomatoes might taste the same, if you only sampled a few pieces the size of dry split peas.

Where and When to Find It   Their acid flavor make these fruits a relatively pleasant trail nibble, when you can find them. Australian saltbush is not common here. I have walked many miles of dikes in Suisun Marsh and noticed this plant in only a few patches. It appears in the Bay Area with a frequency that botanists call occasional, as opposed to common, abundant, or rare.

In addition to Grizzly Island, botanists have found it at one time or another in the following areas: Alviso; Hunter's Point and near Islais Creek in San Francisco; near Greenbrae and San Rafael and in the Mill Valley marsh; and in the East Bay, on landfill near the Bay, as well as in seeps and disturbed areas further inland, such as Corral Hollow and the Altamont Hills.

Who knows? Some late summer or autumn day you may come across this modest plant. If so, by all means taste a fruit, just for the experience. But if you never see it in decades of hiking, don't worry. There are some experiences worth pining for, but tasting Australian saltbush fruits is not one of them.

See also
Fennel Seeds, page 112
Mallow Cheeses, page 118
Mint Leaves, page 192
Rose Hips, page 53

FOR MORE INFORMATION ABOUT FORAGING AND ABOUT PLANTS IN THE BAY AREA

Edible and Useful Plants of California by Charlotte Bringle Clarke (Berkeley: University of California Press, 1977). This excellent, comprehensive guide covers plants from the entire state, with line drawings or photographs for each species.

The Leaf Book by Ida Geary (Fairfield: Tamal Land Press, 1972). Ida Geary is an artist who did beautiful leaf prints from several hundred plants in this area. This is a useful field identification guide that is also lovely in its own right.

Native Shrubs of the San Francisco Bay Region by Roxana S. Ferris (Berkeley: University of California Press, 1968). An indispensable reference for a lover of native plants.

Pacific Coast Berry Finder by Glenn Keator (Berkeley: Nature Study Guild, 1978). This guide to the edible, nonedible, and poisonous berries of California, Oregon, and Washington, has line drawings and range maps for most of the species covered.

Pacific Coast Tree Finder by Tom Watts (Berkeley: Nature Study Guild, 1973). This book has the same arrangement as the berry finder.

Stalking the Wild Asparagus, Stalking the Healthful Herbs, and *Stalking the Blue-Eyed Scallop,* all by Euell Gibbons (New York: David McKay Company, reprinted regularly). These entertaining, enthusiastic books were written about plants in the eastern and central portions of the country, but many of the species occur here, as well. Foragers will find a wealth of detailed information about many common edible species, including numerous recipes.

Trees of North America by C. Frank Brockman (New York: Golden Press, 1968). Only a small fraction of the trees in this book grow in the Bay Area, but since each tree is superbly illustrated with colored paintings of the leaves, and is accompanied by a range map showing where it grows, I find it a useful companion to the *Pacific Coast Tree Finder.*

Thistle Greens and Mistletoe: Edible and Poisonous Plants of Northern California by James Wiltens (Berkeley: Wilderness Press, 1988). Wiltens has collected some entertaining facts about his personal selection of edible plants and drawn them with scientific precision.

If you are interested in a species that's not included in this book and want to know about its distribution in the Bay Area, then you need to use the floras (published lists of the plants in a region). The ones I have found most useful are:

"A Flora of San Francisco, CA" by John Thomas Howell, Peter Raven, and Peter Rubtzoff (*The Wasmann Journal of Biology,* Vol. 16, No. 1, Spring 1958).

A Flora of the San Bruno Mountains, San Mateo County, California by Elizabeth McClintock and Walter Knight (Sacramento: The California Native Plant Society, 1990).

Flora of the Santa Cruz Mountains by John Hunter Thomas (Stanford: Stanford University Press, 1961). Covers San Francisco to Watsonville and Gilroy.

The Flowering Plants and Ferns of Mount Diablo, California by Mary L. Bowerman (Berkeley: The Gillick Press, 1944).

Marin Flora by John Thomas Howell (Berkeley: University of California Press, 1970).

Unfortunately, no one has yet published a flora for Alameda or Contra Costa counties.

At least partial floras have been assembled for some parks, and are available at park headquarters for sale or to read there. Floras have been compiled for Briones, Las Trampas, and Coyote Hills parks, and the East Bay Regional Park District interpretive centers designated for those parks should be able to track them down for you. If you want to know about the vegetation in a particular park, ask a ranger whether a flora has been compiled. There's a good chance that some botany graduate student has done the job.

TREES

Latin Name	Common Name	JAN	FEB	MAR	APR	MAY	JUN	JUL	AUG	SEP	OCT	NOV	DEC
Arbutus menziesii	Madrone			BLOSSOMS			BARK PEELINGS					BERRIES	
Castanopsis chrysophylla	Golden Chinquapin									NUTS			
Corylus cornuta var. californica	California Hazel, Hazelnut, or Wild Filbert						NUTS						
Eucalyptus globulus	Blue Gum Eucalyptus					LEAVES YEAR ROUND							
Ficus species	Fig						FRUIT		FRUIT				
Juglans hindsii	Walnut										NUTS		
Lithocarpus densiflora	Tanoak or Tan Bark Oak									ACORNS			
Malus species	Apple									FRUIT			
Prunus ilicifolia	Holly-leaf Cherry							FRUIT					
Prunus subcordata	Pacific, Klamath, or Sierra Plum						FRUIT						
Prunus species	Plum							FRUIT					
Pseudotsuga menziesii	Douglas Fir					NEEDLES YEAR ROUND							
Pyrus species	Pear									FRUIT			
Quercus agrifolia *Quercus kelloggii* *Quercus lobata*	Coast Live Oak California Black Oak Valley Oak or California White Oak									ACORNS			
Umbellularia californica	California Bay, California Laurel, or Bay Laurel	FLOWERS				LEAVES YEAR ROUND					FRUIT	FLOWERS	NUTS

SHRUBS, SHRUBBY ANNUALS, AND VINES

Latin Name	Common Name	JAN	FEB	MAR	APR	MAY	JUN	JUL	AUG	SEP	OCT	NOV	DEC
Amelanchier pallida	Service Berry or Juneberry								BERRIES / RIPE	DRIED ON BUSH			
Arctostaphylos species	Manzanita							BERRIES					
Artemisia californica	California or Coastal Sagebrush					LEAVES YEAR ROUND							
Berberis nervosa	Oregon Grape or Long-leaf Mahonia							BERRIES					
Berberis pinnata	Shiny-leaf Mahonia												
Eriodictyon californicum	Yerba Santa						LEAVES						
Foeniculum vulgare	Sweet Fennel		STEMS	DRIED SEEDS					GREEN SEEDS			STEMS	DRIED SEEDS
Gaultheria shallon	Salal					LEAVES YEAR ROUND							
Heteromeles arbutifolia (formerly Photinia arbutifolia)	Toyon or Christmas Berry	BERRIES							BERRIES		BERRIES		
Holodiscus discolor	Ocean Spray or Cream Bush					BUDS							
Prunus demissa, also P. virginiana var. demissa	Western Chokecherry							BERRIES					
Ribes californicum	California or Hillside Gooseberry					BERRIES							
Ribes divaricatum	Spreading or Straggly Gooseberry						BERRIES						

SHRUBS, SHRUBBY ANNUALS, AND VINES, continued

Latin Name	Common Name	JAN	FEB	MAR	APR	MAY	JUN	JUL	AUG	SEP	OCT	NOV	DEC
Ribes gracillimum	Bugle or Western Golden Currant						BERRIES						
Ribes malvaceum	Chaparral or California Black Currant					BERRIES							
Ribes menziesii	Canyon Gooseberry								BERRIES				
Ribes sanguineum, also R. glutinosum	Flowering or Pink-flowering Currant						BERRIES						
Rosa californica	California Rose												
Rosa gymnocarpa	Wild or Wood Rose					BLOSSOMS							
Rosa rubiginosa	Sweetbriar or Eglantine Rose								HIPS				
Rosa spithamea	Sonoma Rose												
Rubus discolor (formerly R. procerus)	Himalaya Berry								BERRIES				
Rubus parviflorus	Thimbleberry						BERRIES						
Rubus spectabilis	Salmonberry						BERRIES						
Rubus ursinus	California or Trailing Blackberry								BERRIES				
Sambucus coerula	Blue Elderberry				BLOSSOMS			BERRIES					
Vaccinium ovatum	Evergreen Huckleberry									BERRIES			
Vaccinium parvifolium	Red Huckleberry or Red Bilberry								BERRIES				
Vitis californica	California or Wild Grape										FRUIT		

SMALL PLANTS

Latin Name	Common Name	JAN	FEB	MAR	APR	MAY	JUN	JUL	AUG	SEP	OCT	NOV	DEC
Achillea millefolium	Yarrow				LEAVES								
Allium triquetrum	Wild Onion		BLOSSOMS										
Amaranthus retroflexus	Green Amaranth or Rough Pigweed					LEAVES			SEEDS				
Anthemis cotula	Camomile, Mayweed, or Dog Fennel						BLOSSOMS						
Artemisia douglasiana, A. vulgaris var. heterophylla, and A. ludoviciana	Mugwort						LEAVES						
Asparagus officinalis	Asparagus			SPEARS									
Atriplex hortensis	Garden Orache					LEAVES							
Atriplex patula var. hastata	Fat Hen					LEAVES							
Atriplex semibaccata	Australian Saltbush									FRUIT			
Brassica arvensis	Charlock		LEAVES				BLOSSOMS						
Brassica campestris	Common or Field Mustard		LEAVES					SEEDPODS				LEAVES	
Brassica geniculata	Mediterranean or Summer Mustard												
Brassica kaber, Brassica nigra	Charlock, Black Mustard						LEAVES YEAR ROUND						
Cakile edentula and C. maritima	Sea Rocket												
Capsella bursa-pastoris	Shepherd's Purse			SEEDPODS									

Latin Name	Common Name	JAN	FEB	MAR	APR	MAY	JUN	JUL	AUG	SEP	OCT	NOV	DEC
Carpobrotus chilense (formerly Mesembryanthemum chilense)	Sea Fig									FRUIT			
Carpobrotus edule (formerly Mesembryanthemum edule)	Ice Plant					LEAVES YEAR ROUND				FRUIT			
Chenopodium album	Lamb's Quarters or White Goosefoot				LEAVES				SEEDS				
Chenopodium ambrosioides	Mexican Tea or Epazote						LEAVES						
Cichorium intybus	Chicory			LEAVES									
Erodium cicutarium	Filaree or Storksbill					LEAVES							
Fragaria californica	California or Woodland Strawberry					BERRIES							
Fragaria chiloensis	Coast or Beach Strawberry					BERRIES							
Geranium molle	Cranesbill or Wild Geranium					LEAVES							
Lactuca serriola	Prickly Lettuce	LEAVES											
Lactuca virosa	Wild Lettuce	LEAVES											
Lepidium nitidum	Peppergrass			SEEDPODS									
Malva species	Mallow or Cheeseweed	LEAVES						CHEESES					
Marrubium vulgare	Horehound						LEAVES					LEAVES	

SMALL PLANTS, continued

Latin Name	Common Name	JAN	FEB	MAR	APR	MAY	JUN	JUL	AUG	SEP	OCT	NOV	DEC
Matricaria matricarioides	Pineapple Weed			BLOSSOMS									
Mentha arvensis	Field or Marsh Mint					LEAVES YEAR ROUND							
Mentha citrata	Bergamot Mint												
Mentha piperita	Peppermint												
Mentha pulegium	Pennyroyal												
Mentha rotundifolia	Apple Mint												
Mentha spicata	Spearmint												
Monardella villosa	Coyote Mint or Western Pennyroyal												
Montia perfoliata	Miner's Lettuce		LEAVES										
Nasturtium officinale (formerly Rorippa nasturtium-aquaticum)	Watercress						LEAVES YEAR ROUND						
Oxalis pes-caprae	Oxalis, Sour Grass, or Bermuda Buttercup				BLOSSOMS		LEAVES YEAR ROUND						
Plantago lanceolata	Narrow-leaved Plantain	LEAVES											
Plantago major	Broad-leaved Plantain			LEAVES									
Portulaca oleracea	Purslane or Purselane						LEAVES						
Pteridium aquilinum	Bracken Fern			FIDDLEHEADS									
Raphanus sativus	Wild Radish	LEAVES						BLOSSOMS / SEEDPODS					
Rumex acetosella	Sheep Sorrel						LEAVES YEAR ROUND						
Rumex crispus	Curly Dock		LEAVES										

SMALL PLANTS, continued

Latin Name	Common Name	JAN	FEB	MAR	APR	MAY	JUN	JUL	AUG	SEP	OCT	NOV	DEC
Salicornia virginica	Pickleweed					STEMS							
Satureja chamissonis	Yerba Buena			LEAVES YEAR ROUND									LEAVES
Sonchus oleraceus	Sow Thistle		LEAVES								LEAVES		
Stellaria media	Chickweed	LEAVES											
Taraxacum officinale	Dandelion					LEAVES YEAR ROUND							
Tetragonia tetragonioides	New Zealand Spinach					LEAVES YEAR ROUND							
Trifolium repens	White Clover						BLOSSOMS						
Trifolium pratense	Red Clover						LEAVES						
Tropaeolum majus	Nasturtium			LEAVES				BLOSSOMS					
Typha species	Cattail	SPURS / SHOOTS / GREEN BLOSSOM SPIKES / POLLEN / ROOTS YEAR ROUND											
Urtica holosericea	Hoary Nettle		LEAVES										
Urtica urems	Dwarf Nettle												

MUSHROOMS

Latin Name	Common Name	JAN	FEB	MAR	APR	MAY	JUN	JUL	AUG	SEP	OCT	NOV	DEC
Agaricus augustus	The Prince												
Cantharellus cibarius	Chanterelle												
Lepista nuda	Blewitt												
Pleurotus ostreatus	Oyster Mushroom												

SEAWEEDS

Latin Name	Common Name	JAN	FEB	MAR	APR	MAY	JUN	JUL	AUG	SEP	OCT	NOV	DEC
Ahnfeltia gigartinoides	Nibbles		█	█	█	█	█	█	█	█			
Alaria marginata	Alaria						█	█	█	█	█		
Analipus japonicus	Sea Fir or Fir Needles			█	█	█	█	█	█	█	█		
Cystoseira osmundacea	Sister Sarah					█	█	█					
Enteromorpha clathrata	Stone Hair			█	█								
Enteromorpha intestinales	Green Nori												
Fucus vesiculosis	Bladderwrack or Rockweed			█	█	█	█	█	█	█			
Gigartina exasperata	Turkish Bath Towel												
Gracilaria verrucosa	Ogo					█	█	█	█				
Halosaccion glandiforme	Sea Sac					█	█	█					
Iridaea cordata	Iridaea					█	█	█	█	█	█		
Laminaria sinclairii	Laminaria or Kombu			█	█	█	█	█	█	█			
Nereocystis luetkeana	Bull Whip Kelp						█	█	█				
Petalonia fascia	Sea Petals or Flower Seaweed					█	█	█			█		
Petrocelis middendorffii (formerly *Gigartina papillata*)	Grapestone												
Porphyra lanceolata	Nori					█	█	█	█	█	█		
Porphyra perforata	Laver or Nori					█	█	█	█				
Ulva lactuca	Sea Lettuce					█	█	█	█				

INDEX

Achillea millefolium, 176–177, 179
Actaea species, 15
Aesculus californica, 14
Agaricus augustus, 144, 145
Ahnfeltia gigartinoides, 173
Alaria, 155–157
Alaria marginata, 155–157
Allium triquetrum, 25, 35–36
Amaranth, green, 115
Amaranthus retroflexus, 115
Amelanchier pallida, 69–71
Analipus japonicus, 173
Anthemis cotula, 190–191
Apple, 47–49
Arbutus menziesii, 38–41, 92
Arctostaphylos species, 41–43
Artemisia californica, 12, 177–178, 179
A. douglasiana, 179–182
A. ludoviciana, 179–182
A. vulgaris var. heterophylla, 179–182
Asparagus, 24, 100–101
Asparagus officinalis, 24, 100–101
Atriplex hortensis, 114
A. patula var. hastata, 114
A. semibaccata, 208–209
Baneberry, 15
Bay, California, 9, 85, 92, 145, 146, 199–202
Bay laurel. See Bay, California
Berberis nervosa, 71–72
B. pinnata, 71–72
Bladderwrack, 159–160
Blackberry, California or trailing, 5, 57–59, 77
Blewitt, 146
Blue gum eucalyptus, 99, 186–187
Blue witch, 23
Bracken fern, 102–103
Brassica arvensis, 25, 26–31, 96
B. campestris, 25, 26–31, 96
B. geniculata, 25, 26–31, 96
B. kaber, 25, 26–31, 96
B. nigra, 25, 26–31, 96
Buckeye, California, 14
Bull whip kelp, 168–169
Buttercup, 32
Cakile edentula, 129–130
C. maritima, 129–130
Cantharellus cibarius, 144, 145
Capsella bursa-pastoris, 207–208
Carpobrotus chilense, 46–47
C. edule, 46–47
Castanopsis chrysophylla, 85–86
Cattail, 12, 104–107
Chamomile, 190–191
Chanterelle, 144, 145

Charlock, 25, 26–31, 96
Cheeseweed, 118–119
Chenopodium album, 95, 116–117
C. ambrosioides, 182–183
Cherry, holly-leaf, 75–76
Chicory, 109–110
Chickweed, 11, 18, 107–108
Chinquapin, golden, 85–86
Chokecherry, western, 74–75
Christmas berry, 80–82
Cichorium intybus, 109–110
Cicuta species, 16
Clover
  red, 198–199
  white, 198–199
Coffee berry, 79
Conium maculatum, 6, 14, 16–18, 100, 101, 107–108, 113
Corylus cornuta var. californica, 83, 84–85
Cotoneaster species, 81
Cranesbill, 136–137
Cream bush, 204
Cucumber, wild, 21
Curly dock, 110–111, 120
Currants
  bugle or western golden, 49–51
  chaparral or California black, 49–51
  flowering or pink-flowering, 49–51
Cystoseira osmundacea, 157–158
Dandelion, 135–136
Desmarestia species, 152–153
Dock, curly, 110–111, 120
Douglas fir, 40, 145, 196–197, 200
Elderberry
  blue, 60–63
  red, 60–61
Enteromorpha clathrata, 174
E. intestinalis, 158–159, 174
Epazote, 182–183
Eriodictyon californicum, 4, 12, 183–185
Erodium cicutarium, 136–137
Eucalyptus, blue gum, 99, 186–187
Eucalyptus globulus, 99, 186–187
Fat hen, 114
Fennel
  dog, 190–191
  sweet, 18, 100, 101, 112–113
Fern, bracken, 102–103
Ficus species, 47–49
Fig, 47–49
Filaree, 136–137
Filberts, wild, 83, 84–85
Fir, Douglas, 40, 145, 196, 200
Fir needles, 173
Flower seaweed, 173
Foeniculum vulgare, 18, 100, 101, 112–113

Fragaria californica, 44–46
F. chiloensis, 44–46
Fucus vesiculosis, 159–160
Garrya elliptica, 19, 74
G. fremontii, 19, 74
Gaultheria shallon, 72–74
Geranium molle, 136–137
Geranium, wild, 136–137
Gigartina papillata, 161–163, 166
G. exasperata, 161–163
Gooseberries
  California or hillside, 49–52
  canyon, 49–52
  spreading or straggly, 49–52
Goosefoot, white, 95, 116–117
Gracilaria verrucosa, 164–165
Grape, California or wild, 68–69
Grapestone, 161–163, 166
Green nori, 158–159, 174
Halosaccion glandiforme, 174
Hazel, California, 83, 84–85
Hazelnut, 83, 84–85
Hemlock
  poison, 6, 14, 16–18, 100, 101, 107–108, 113
  water, 16
Heteromeles arbutifolia, 80–82
Himalaya berry, 57–59
Holly-leaf cherry, 75–76
Holodiscus discolor, 204
Horehound, 188–189
Huckleberry
  evergreen, 64–68, 78
  red, 78
Ice plant, 46–47
Iridaea, 166
Iridaea cordata, 166
Juglans hindsii, 84, 93–94
Juneberry, 69–71
Kelp, bull whip, 168–169
Kombu, 167
Lactuca serriola, 117–118
L. virosa, 117–118
Lamb's quarters, 95, 116–117
Laminaria, 167
Laminaria sinclairii, 167
Laurel, California, 9, 85, 92, 145, 146, 199–202
Laver, 169–170
Lettuce
  miner's, 9, 11, 96–99, 120
  prickly, 117–118
  sea, 158, 171–172
  wild, 117–118
Lepidium nitidum, 205–206
Lepista nuda, 146
Lithocarpus densiflora, 40, 87–92, 145, 146
Lonicera involucrata, 80
Lupine, 20
Lupinus species, 20
Madrone, 38–41, 92
Mahonia
  long-leaf, 71–72
  shiny-leaf, 71–72
Mallow, 118–119

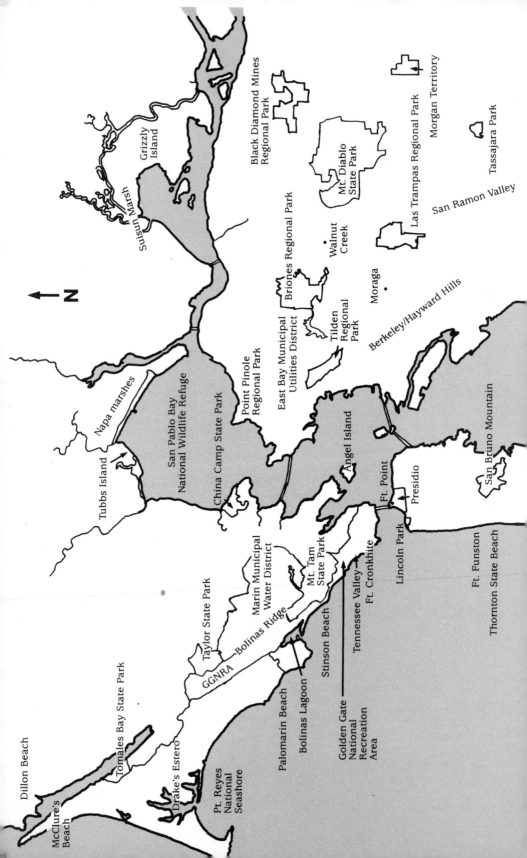

N ←

Dillon Beach

McClure's Beach

Tomales Bay State Park

Drake's Estero

Pt. Reyes National Seashore

Palomarin Beach

Bolinas Lagoon

Bolinas Ridge

GGNRA

Taylor State Park

Marin Municipal Water District

Mt. Tam State Park

Stinson Beach

Tennessee Valley

Golden Gate National Recreation Area

Ft. Cronkhite

Lincoln Park

Ft. Point

Presidio

Ft. Funston

Thornton State Beach

San Bruno Mountain

Angel Island

Tubbs Island

Napa marshes

San Pablo Bay National Wildlife Refuge

China Camp State Park

Point Pinole Regional Park

East Bay Municipal Utilities District

Briones Regional Park

Tilden Regional Park

Suisun Marsh

Grizzly Island

Black Diamond Mines Regional Park

Mt. Diablo State Park

Walnut Creek

Moraga

Berkeley/Hayward Hills

Las Trampas Regional Park

Morgan Territory

Tassajara Park

San Ramon Valley

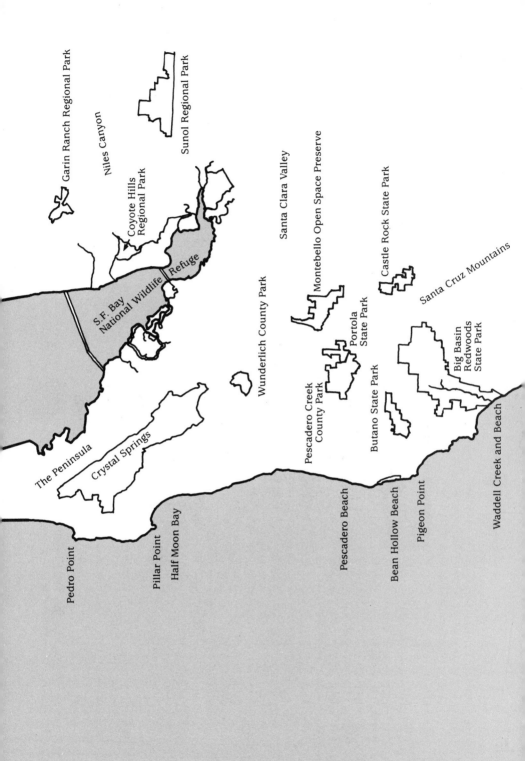

ABOUT THE AUTHOR

Margit Roos-Collins is an environmental compliance lawyer at Heller, Ehrman, White & McAuliffe in San Francisco. She was educated at Princeton University and Boston University School of Law. When she was six months old, she moved to Riverside, California, where her parents would push her carriage through orange groves after storms and pile windfall oranges in beside her. Maybe it all began there. When the citrus groves were cut down and the mountains were no longer visible, her family moved East, but she found her way back to California in 1976. She lives in the Bay Area with her husband, Richard Roos-Collins. *The Flavors of Home* is her first book.

ABOUT THE ILLUSTRATOR

Rose Craig is an artist who lives in Berkeley, California, and has illustrated natural history and outdoor sports books for national and local publishers. She is also a photographer, painter, and cartoonist, and is currently using all of these media in the Exhibits and Design Department at UC Berkeley's Lawrence Hall of Science.